AN

MW01204470

MYTHOLOGY

Discover the Secrets of Ancient Greece and Greek Mythology

Martin R. Phillips

PART 1

ANCIENT GREECE

PART 2

GREEK MYTHOLOGY

PART **1**
ANCIENT GREECE

Discovering Ancient Greece

INTRODUCTION

Ancient Greece is, without a doubt, one of the most fascinating cultures that our world has ever seen! Whether you look at their mythology, their history, or their philosophy, the Ancient Greek civilization has permeated our approach to, and understanding of, the world at large. It is impossible to tell the story of modern civilization without providing some recognition to the influence of Greece.

The Greek Empire was vast, encompassing over 700 individual city-states, 150-173 of which would form the Delian League in an effort to combat the onslaught of Persia. How did so many city-states come together under one rule? With only a fraction joining the Delian League, how did these city-states *stay* together in times of disagreement and conflict?

There are hundreds, if not thousands of questions regarding this vast and fascinating civilization. One could spend years and write many volumes on each period of the Ancient Grecian culture, history, and mythology. It has been my pleasure to assemble this research, and the voice of Greece itself (through reference to its own historians, including Herodotus,

Thucydides, and Xenophon.) I am excited to share with you an admittedly brief look at the civilization we know as Ancient Greece (a full history would take more pages than the unabridged Oxford English Dictionary and the Encyclopedia Britannica combined.)

In this book you will find the history and opinions of the Ancient Greeks. You will discover their truth and their mythology. You will learn of war and peacetime. There are heroes and villains, saints and scoundrels. You will find philosophies that changed the world, and continue to do so even to this day.

For the most part, the contents of this book are arranged topically as opposed to strictly chronologically to allow specific areas of interest in the Ancient Greeks and their civilization to be more easily accessible. However, care has been taken to include the approximate dates of people and events to give you a good idea of the chronology of the content.

The importance of the Greek civilization cannot be overstated. In nearly every facet of our lives, we can find something which had its roots, or took a new turn in Ancient Greece. When you go to the polls to elect an official, you are operating on a Greek principle. When you discuss the nature of life with others, you are performing a modified version of the Greek symposium. Even when you sit down to watch television, or read a book, you often find references to Trojan wars, Sparta and their role in the conflict with the

Persians, the philosophy, or the character of the Greeks.

As you rediscover Ancient Greece, I encourage you to make note of how much of that vast and diverse civilization still lives on throughout our world today.

Thanks again, I hope you enjoy it!

CHAPTER 1

The Beginning

While the earliest portions of what would come to be ancient Greece are largely lost to antiquity, there is still quite a bit that we can deduce from the evidence that we do have.

The era commonly known as ancient Greece began in the 8th century BC and lasted until around the 7th century AD with the end of antiquity. Ancient Greece consisted of a few distinct periods of Greek government and culture. These include the Archaic, Classical, Hellenistic, and Roman periods.

This chapter, however, will give you a brief outline of the time period preceding that of what we commonly call Ancient Greece. Points of focus include: The Neolithic Era, The Bronze Age including the Minoan, Cycladic, and Mycenaean civilizations, and the Greek Dark Age.

The Neolithic Era: 6,800-3,200 BC

While there was activity in the area which would come to be known as Ancient Greece before these periods, The Neolithic era saw the stabilization of the climate, the introduction of farming, stock-rearing, and pottery; and the building of settlements among other important matters.

The last Glacial Period (inaccurately termed the last Ice Age) ended around 8,000 BC, and this led to the advent of more permanent settlements in Greece. Prior to this period, many peoples were nomadic, but with the stabilization of the climate, they were able to build these permanent settlements.

The economy was largely based on a barter system where goods and services were traded for produce from farmers, cattle and other stock, and pottery. This diversification allowed people to focus more on one particular kind of work as they could barter their trade for whatever provisions they needed.

Settlement and the meeting of an individual's daily needs (food, water, etc.) led to the advent of craftsmen. These people were specialists in their particular areas, and trade became a more important facet of everyday life. People turned to outside sources to supplement things which were either unavailable, or in short supply in their given areas, and everyone was able to meet their essential needs without the necessity of traveling from place to place. Neolithic settlements were often fortified, but allowed trade and travel for its citizens.

Although hunting and gathering provided individuals with much more free time than agriculture has, it was also much less efficient. It would take about 1,000 calories of expenditure to obtain 1,000 calories of food, thus surplus was relatively unheard of. People had to move from place to place as nomads in order to ensure that they could hunt and gather enough food to sustain them.

The Neolithic Age is often known as the last period of the Stone Age. Tools were usually made of stone, as well as weapons, building materials, and other necessities as it was extremely plentiful in all areas of the habitable world.

The advent of agriculture, often known as either the agricultural revolution or The Neolithic Revolution, allowed people to remain in one place and actually obtain a surplus of food. Having a food surplus allowed settlements to grow and, although without agriculture people had more time, less use for slave labor, very little impact on their (and subsequently) our environment, Ancient Greece, let alone modern civilization would be impossible in the way we know it.

Aegean Civilization (The Greek Bronze Age): 3,200-1,050 BC

The Aegean civilization is a reference to The Bronze Age settlements of Greece in and around the Aegean Sea. The Aegean Bronze Age started around 3,200 BC, (Aegean Islands around 3,000 BC, and Crete in about 2,800 BC,) although there is a great deal of speculation on the exact dates. Initially, bronze was very expensive, and so it was typically reserved for the wealthy. In fact, the class system of civilization was largely initiated based on the availability of these metals, and who had them.

Due to its initially limited supply, bronze took quite a while to become commonplace, but was generally in use beginning around 2,800 BC. What led to its popularity and widespread use was the fact that bronze was much easier to use than traditional tools, and thus it eventually replaced stone for tools and weapons.

In Greece, The Bronze Age was typified by the expansion of settlements, the development of navigation, the growth of individual dwellings, and further class stratification. During this time, trade became more and more vital to the growth and sustainability of cities and thus found great expansion.

There were three predominant groups in the area of Greece during this time. They were the Minoan, the Cycladic, and the Mycenaean civilizations.

The Cycladic civilization existed from approx. 3,200-2,000 BC. The Cycladic civilization was located on a number of islands in the Aegean Sea, most notably around the Cyclades. Although not much is known about the inner-workings of this civilization, we do have archaeological evidence which suggests that they were seafaring people who were notable for sculpture. Some evidence shows signs of copper-working. Their sculptures have been found in various places in the Greek area, including Knossos on the island of Crete. With the exception of Delos, this group drifted into the background with the advent of Cretan palace-culture.

Like the Cyclades, there isn't much specific knowl-edge of the Minoan civilization. In fact, the term Mi-noan was coined by Arthur Evans, and is taken from the mythical King Minos, a son of Zeus and Europa. The Minoans controlled many of the Greek Islands, most notably Crete

The Minoan Civilization on Crete lasted from approx. 2,700 BC to 1,450 BC, and began in the city of Knos-sos. The island was rich in natural resources, and the Minoans took great part in overseas trading. They were largely merchants and fishermen, although they made use of lumber for trading and building their sea craft. There were craftsmen, and traders, indicating a proliferation of craft specialization. The Minoan civilization of Crete was invaded by the Mycenaeans in about 1,400 BC. Their written language is known as Linear A, and is presently indecipherable.

The Mycenaeans, often referred to as "Proto-Greeks," were a Helladic (of mainland Greece) civilization from approx. 1,600-1,050 BC, although they did come to control many of the Greek Islands during the span of their civilization. They did speak an early form of Greek and had two predominant forms of written language known as Linear A and Linear B. While Linear B was largely deciphered in the 1950s, Linear A remains indecipherable. As there are no written historical accounts that we're presently aware of about the Mycenaeans *by* the Mycenaeans, historians have been able to trace their culture through by tracking their pottery.

The Mycenaeans get their name from archaeologists of the 19th century from the name of their capitol city of Mycenae, which is located about 56 miles (90 kilometers) southwest of Athens. Mycenae is also well-known for being the city from which the mythical Agamemnon ruled in Homer's Iliad. In The Iliad, the Trojan wars were fought between the peoples of Mycenae and the city of Troy. The storyline of the Greek poet Homer The Iliad beginning nine years after the beginning of the mythical Trojan War.

The Mycenaeans were bold traders, fierce warriors, and phenomenal engineers made up of numerous cities connected by a common language and culture. The people were governed by a singular king who had ultimate power to levy taxes, and generally govern the people. These kings were extremely wealthy

Mycenaean buildings were usually built atop a hill and were made of stone, both of which suggest that they were designed with defense in mind. Some of these structures are still standing today, including the Lion's Gate in Mycenae.

The economy was a palace-economy, a moneyless system where goods are stored in a central location and doled out to the people as needed. These goods were largely the products of farming and trade.

The collapse of the Mycenaean civilization occurred sometime between 1,200 and 1,050 BC. The reasons for the collapse are unknown; however the cities of this civilization were either abandoned or, in many cases, destroyed. Speculation about the collapse includes rebellion, invasion, or possibly a widespread natural disaster.

The Greek Dark Ages (or Early Iron Age) 1,200-800 BC

This period in Greece was largely characterized by the loss of cities and a great loss of writing. However the culture may have lost many of its important facets, iron working began to come about, and iron would eventually replace bronze as the predominant metal of tools and weapons, etc.

With the loss of cities, many of the people relied upon herding to fulfill their needs. The surplus of food had largely dissipated with the dissolution of the Mycenaean civilization and their many cities.

At some point between 1,100 and 950 BC, something often referred to as The Dorian Invasion occurred. The Dorian Invasion is a term often used to explain the transition between the pre-classical language, writing and culture to that which was predominant in classical Greece, specifically the area around Sparta.

The classical mythos behind this event is that the descendants of Hercules returned to reclaim the lands which Hercules had held during his lifetime. Much more likely is that it wasn't an actual invasion at all, but a migration which occurred over a very long period of time.

CHAPTER 2

The Pantheon of the Gods

To understand what the religion of Ancient Greece was to its people is to understand a great deal about the people themselves. These gods and goddesses along with the mythos attached to them would dominate Greek knowledge and philosophy for centuries.

The Greek Religion was polytheistic (belief in multiple gods) and these gods were said to interact with people on a constant basis. Many women would claim that they had gotten pregnant through intercourse with one of the chief deities, often Zeus himself. Others claimed that their injuries or diseases were cured by the gods' own intervention. Still more attributed military victories, social and political success, acts of nature, and various other positive and negative personal or collective experiences to the intervention of these gods.

Rather than simply provide a list of the gods and their attributions, it seems fitting to give a closer account of the chief gods and their powers, their hierarchical structure, and effects on Ancient Greek civilization. Along with the gods themselves, the religion, morality, and general mythology bear investigation.

The gods were not the omnipotent, ambivalently benevolent gods which dominate the cultural landscape today. The gods behaved and appeared much more like the people who worshipped them. The gods weren't just jealous of the others, they were also believed to engage in (consensual and nonconsensual) sexual intercourse on a regular basis, and had the same human emotions and imperfections as the people who worshipped them.

There was a power structure to the pantheon with Zeus as its king. Zeus was the youngest son of Cronus and Rhea and had a modicum of control over all of the other gods. However, many myths and legends have the other gods sneaking around behind Zeus's back and causing all sorts of mischief. Zeus controlled the weather, and wielded lightning bolts. He is said to have ruled the Olympians (in this case, the inhabitant gods of Olympus) as a father ruled his family.

Although in most traditions Zeus is married to Hera, his frequent sexual exploits resulted in his various children with other deities and, quite often, with mortal women as well as in the case of Heracles (often called Hercules.) In most instances of his intercourse with goddesses, the children were born as new gods or goddesses such as Athena, Hermes, and Ares (to name a brief few.) His affairs with mortal women, however, often resulted in beings such as Heracles who were a hybrid of hero and god.

The gods of the ancient Greeks often presided over various functions of nature, such as Helios as the god who controlled the movement of the sun; and Poseidon who ruled over the sea. Other times, the gods were behind different emotions or states of being such as Aphrodite who ruled over love; and Uranus who was the god of the sky, or the heavens.

Other notable entities included the primordial gods such as Chaos, the father of life, the universe, etc.; and Aether who was the god of the pure upper air of the Olympians (not to be confused with the normal air that mortals breathe.)

There were the Titans who were a powerful race of gods who spawned (and were subsequently overthrown by) the Olympians such as Mnemosyne who was the personification of memory and was mother to the muses; and Cronus (often Kronos) who was the father of Zeus and led the revolt against Uranus (the sky.)

Cronus is particularly of interest in Greek mythology in that he feared losing power to his children as his father had lost power to him. He therefore ate five of his six children one by one. The sixth child, Zeus, was saved by his mother (Cronus's wife and sister) Rhea when, after Zeus's birth, she presented a stone to Cronus, swaddled in cloth so that he would be unaware that he was not consuming his new son. When Zeus grew up, he forced Cronus to imbibe a potion which caused the latter to vomit up the children which he had devoured. Thus, his siblings were reborn. The siblings: Demeter, Hestia, Hera, Hades, Poseidon and Zeus joined together to wage war against their father and the rest of the Titans, eventually bound and launched into oblivion.

Other gods and godlike beings included The Muses who were said to be the goddesses of inspiration. There were Nymphs who were divine beings who animated different aspects of nature. There were the Giants, and their relatives the Cyclopes who were one-eyed giants. Along with these, there were also various beings consisting of half-humans or human-like beings such as satyrs (half-man and half-goat,) centaurs (half-man and half horse,) and gorgons (hideous female creatures with hair made of live, venomous snakes,) of which Medusa is a well-known example.

Many books could be and have been written about the various gods, titans, etc. What is important is how the belief in these gods affected the Greeks in their culture and in their daily lives.

Greek morality was largely based on striving toward moderation, as most vices were considered acceptable in-and-of themselves, while taking these things to extremes, such as overeating, excessive drinking, etc. would lead one to great error.

Hubris (extreme pride to the point of delusion) was the most feared and despised of vices, as it was seen as a chief cause behind things such as rape, murder, and betrayal. Pride itself wasn't considered a negative thing, however when it reached the point of hubris, it had reached the point of being out of control, and was often personified as pridefulness and an overestimation of one's abilities to the exclusion of others' rights.

Many of the Greek city-states were based upon a belief that a particular deity was the city's patron. Who the people chose as their city-state's patron shows a lot about the focus of that city-state. Athens for instance was named for their patron goddess Athena. The city was therefore primarily concerned with education and knowledge, as Athena was the goddess of wisdom. Sparta had two: Ares, and Artemis. Ares, the god of war signified Sparta's focus on military might while Artemis, the god of the hunt among other things.

Many of the Greek myths were used to explain natural phenomena. One such myth is that of Persephone and Hades. It was said that Persephone, the unspeakably gorgeous daughter of Demeter, goddess of fertility, was working in a field one day when the earth cracked open, and she was taken to the underworld by Hades. For nine days, Demeter searched for her daughter, neglecting the crops of the earth which caused them to die off. Zeus, seeing that humanity could not survive without Demeter to make the earth fertile again, intervened, and demanded that Hades release Persephone to be with her mother. Hades agreed to release Persephone so long as she hadn't eaten anything while in the underworld. However, Hades had tricked Persephone into eating pomegranate seeds. It was finally decided that while Persephone would be allowed to live with her mother during most of the year, she would have to return to Hades for three months. During the time in which Persephone was with her mother, crops flourished; however during her three months with Hades, the world became cold and barren. Such was the explanation for winter.

The Olympic Games were originally established to pay tribute to Zeus. Along with these games, which were held in the city of Olympia, animals were sacrificed to Zeus. Priests would then take the blood of the slaughtered animals and spread it on an altar in the temple of Zeus to further honor their deity.

One more tradition in Greek religion was the development of mystery schools. These schools or cults were each dedicated to a particular deity. For instance, the Eleusinian mystery school was a cult of Demeter. Anyone who had clean hands, in other words had not committed a blood offense such as murder, was allowed entry; however communication with anyone outside who was uninitiated was strictly forbidden. An example of how serious this secrecy was occurred when two teenage boys were caught spying on the rites of the Eleusinian cult. The punishment for those boys was death.

CHAPTER 3

The Birth of Democracy

Moving from mythology back to historical fact, we come to the Athenian Revolution in 508 BC. The people, who had been oppressed for hundreds of years by those in power, revolted against their rulers. The people would find the solution to their trials in one of the most unlikely people.

There are two common approaches to the Athenian Revolution, and both will be taken here in the interest of covering the topic as thoroughly as possible, as this conflict and its resulting governmental changes would change the way that Greece, and subsequently the world, would approach politics. One is to focus on Cleisthenes himself, the other is to look more at the character of the people who fought for their freedom.

Cleisthenes, born around 570 BC, was an aristocrat who, like others of his ilk, had been brought up to be a ruler. He was a descendant of Cleisthenes of Sicyon, a tyrant. The term tyrant in those days didn't neces-

sarily denote corruption; rather it described an absolute ruler. Cleisthenes was born and brought up in a
palatial home, and was reared with the belief that
certain privileges were his by right of his noble birth.

The political climate of Greece during this time period was largely a struggle between city-states to gain
land or influence from another. Oftentimes a polis
(city-state) would be struggling for its independence
from another. Although many aspects of the Greek
city-states were shared, such as the overall religion,
there was no common system of governance, and
each polis was under its own ruler(s).

Athens in the early days of Cleisthenes, as well as
during the Athenian revolution was a relatively small
polis which was led by an individual tyrant. The
tyrant whose corruption led the Athenians to their
historical revolt was Hippias, son of Peisistratus
(Cleisthenes's brother-in-law.)

Peisistratus came to power in Athens by having an
especially tall girl from a neighboring village accom-
pany him to Athens. He claimed that she was Athena
herself, and demanded that he be given rule of the
polis. The people welcomed him as their ruler. Peisistratus, in order to ensure his continued power over
the polis of Athens, appealed to the common people.
He offered the people prosperity by lowering taxes
and doling out free loans, not only to ensure that the

people were in his favor, but also to build up the polis itself.

Under the rule of Peisistratus, Athens was transformed from a smaller rural polis into a center of trade and innovation. The rule of Peisistratus was a great departure from the aristocracy which had dominated Athens and, indeed, most of Greece during this time. Upon his death, tyranny (the rule) of Athens was passed to Peisistratus's son, Hippias.

Hippias began his career much in step with that of his father's rule. He ruled with a modicum of respect and good-treatment of the people of Athens. However, when his brother was murdered, Hippias became paranoid and vitriolic against the people of Athens. He began to execute and banish people who either were, or who he thought were connected with his brother's murder. He took the new freedoms that the people had gained under Peisistratus and replaced it with oppression.

Cleisthenes began his involvement in the revolution of Athens around 510 BC with the intention of seizing power for himself. He had been brought up to further his self-interest, and followed this dictum to its end. Cleisthenes conspired, and succeeded in overthrowing Hippias, and the latter was banished from Athens.

The rule of Cleisthenes was, however, beset by its own conspirators and rivals. The chief rival of Cleisthenes was another Athenian aristocrat named Isagoras. Isagoras had long been involved with the Spartans, and was even rumored to have shared his wife with the king of Sparta. Isagoras appealed to the Spartans to aid him in deposing Cleisthenes, and the Spartans complied.

Sparta, which is most well known for its military prowess, was poised to make Athens a subject of its growing realm of influence. The warlike polis had already dominated its surrounding area for hundreds of square miles, and with Isagoras, a friend of Sparta, as the new ruler of Athens, its influence was set to grow even more.

Fearing the opposition of Cleisthenes and other aristocrats, Isagoras banished Cleisthenes from Athens along with some 700 other households, and it looked like he may never return to his home again. However, having had a taste of freedom under the rule of Peisistratus, the people of Athens revolted against Isagoras and his Spartan allies.

Isagoras and his forces sought refuge in The Acropolis for a period of two days. On the third day, however, he surrendered to the onslaught of the common Athenian people. The citizens of Athens had taken power from the despot (absolute ruler) and had claimed it for themselves. The year was 508 BC. The people recalled Cleisthenes, and the others who had been banished by Isagoras.

It was clear that Cleisthenes could not rule in the manner which had been so common in Athens and various other Greek city-states of the time. It had become apparent that the people must be able to have a say in how they were governed. Cleisthenes ordered a stone meeting area to be carved out of the rock some distance from The Acropolis where the people of the city, commoners and aristocrats alike, could meet and discuss the issues of Athens. It was here that Cleisthenes instituted a simple form of voting. The first instances of the voting process consisted of presenting a white pebble to indicate assent, and a black pebble to indicate disagreement with whatever proposal was before the people.

Issues were brought for a vote every nine days, and these issues encompassed every facet of governance in the polis. This was a pure democracy where the government was one of the people without a separate body to counter or inhibit the decision of the people. Issues such as the declaration of war, raising or lowering taxes, all the way down to the prices of produce and other goods were decided by these democratic votes.

Not only would the advent of democracy give the common people as much of a say in the nature and direction of their government, it would create a system which would change the way that people of the area, and indeed the world after it, would view people's rights, and responsibilities in their own governance. Forms of democracy are still present today, and in its purest forms, it gives people the ability to have an actual, not only a perceived say, in what the government does.

While larger governments that take on a semblance of democracy today often rely heavily on the ideas of a republic (a system where officials are either elected or appointed to represent their individual areas such as representatives in the United States, or members of The House of Commons in Britain,) for the day to day issues and votes, as it would be wildly inefficient to hold votes with the general population every time an issue was presented, the earliest Greek democracy was a direct democracy which did incorporate this widespread influence of the people in every facet of governmental affairs.

The rise of democracy in Athens paved the way for the golden age of Greece. Culture after the advent of democracy in Athens and, subsequently, the rest of Greece flourished in a way that it never had before this time period.

There is evidence of other proto-democratic governments prior to the advent of Athenian democracy, however, the system instituted by Cleisthenes and his fellows was certainly the first of its kind. Not everyone in Athens had the right to vote however. Voting was intended only for adult males, although it's suspected that a voter's family may have had a good deal of influence on his vote.

Another influence that reached voters in a dramatic way (no pun intended) was the satire of the comedic poets of the time. These poets, like artists today, found the ability to sway public opinion in a very real way, and they would often use this power to turn votes to favor their own opinions.

Democracy, although popular among a good share of the people, was considered to be fallacious by many including the great philosopher Plato. Plato believed that unless elected officials were philosophers of the finest thread, Greece would never be free of the evils of ambition and tyranny. Plato favored a kingdom ruled by men of philosophy to ensure continual progress and rescue from the necessary evils contained in men who failed to question.

Another interesting facet of Athenian democracy was that of ostracism. Ostracism, put simply, was the voted ejection of a person from the borders of the city-state. Although the practice had the potential to rid the area of individuals who would be counterproductive to the spread of Greek freedoms, it was often used as a political tool to oust individuals who were unliked by an individual or a group. This process was often unofficially sanctioned for such means, as in the case of Themistocles, the great general who had led the Athenians to many important victories against Persia.

Although Athenian democracy wasn't perfect, it undoubtedly led to the Golden Age of Greece. People were brought together more through this simple invention, the casting of a stone, than they had been in the previous history of the land. Not only culture, but trade, production, the economy, and many other facets of Greek life were enhanced by this revolutionary concept.

CHAPTER 4

Darius, Xerxes, and the Persian Threat

In 492 BC, though the Democracy of Athens was still very young, Athens began to gain a significant amount of power. Athens at the time was still a smaller polis, but it caught the attention of Darius, known as The Great King of The Persian Empire.

The Persian Empire was undoubtedly the greatest power of the day. It was located across the sea to the East of Athens, and stretched from Turkey all the way to India. The Empire was ruled by Darius, a tyrannical leader who demanded unyielding submission. Darius was so feared by his people, and had such a level of dominion over them that those who would beg his favor were required to cover their mouths when in his presence so the air that he breathed would not be contaminated by their presence.

As all dictatorial rulers do, Darius feared the growth in power of any civilization other than his own. When it became clear that Athens was becoming too powerful for Darius's liking, he sent a force to invade.

The first campaign of the Persians against the Greeks was carried out by Mardonius, the son-in-law of Darius. During this campaign, Mardonius's forces conquered and re-subjugated the city of Thrace. Macedon, an ally of the Persians, was also subjugated. This campaign, although having its victories would end after the Persian fleet was lost in a storm near the coast of Mount Athos. After being injured during a raid of his camp, Mardonius returned home.

Darius sent ambassadors to all of the poleis of Greece demanding submission to his rule in 491, and almost all of these city-states complied. In Sparta and Athens, however, not only were the ambassadors refused their submission, but were also killed.

Undoubtedly the most famous event of the war between Darius's Persia and the city-states of Greece was the battle of Marathon. The Persians landed in the polis of Marathon, a city which had no standing army. News of the Persian invasion travelled quickly. The Persian Empire was one of tyranny and slavery, while the Greek city-states were a culture which valued its freedom.

That being so, a herald (or day runner/courier) named Pheidippides was sent from Athens to request the aid of Sparta, the military superpower of the Greek poleis, in dispelling the Persian force from their shores. Pheidippides ran over 150 miles (246 kilometers) in the space of less than two days. This remarkable journey through the countryside of Greece is the origin of modern marathons.

Although Pheidippides performed an astonishing feat by making this desperate run, the Spartans refused the plea for help. Athens would have to defend itself against the Persians.

While Pheidippides was making his run, the Athenians were gathering their forces. Everyone who was able from peasants armed with spears, sticks, or whatever they could find to the hoplites who were citizen-soldiers, able to afford the finer armor. The hoplites were predominantly armed with spears, clad in armor of bronze, and generally had some military training.

Despite being outnumbered two-to-one by the Persian forces, the Greek soldiers won an unlikely victory against their invaders. They killed an estimated 6,000 Persian troops in one day, and scattered their forces.

The victory of the Greeks over the Persians was an incredible blow to Darius. After the loss to the Greeks in the failed first invasion, Darius began amassing yet another enormous army. This army was intended to invade Greece yet again, but it fell into discord when the Egyptians revolted. Darius died while trying to quell this uprising. With Darius's death in 486 BC, control of The Persian Empire was passed to his son Xerxes.

Xerxes was hateful toward the Greeks and the Egyptians, blaming them for the death of his father. The revolt in Egypt was quickly put down by Xerxes, and a new plan to invade Greece was initiated. He decided to bridge Hellespont (modern day Dardanelles) a thin sea strait about .75 miles (1.2 kilometers) at its thinnest point in order for his massive army to cross into Greece.

Many of the Greek poleis pledged to voluntarily join with Xerxes and the Persian Empire when the Persians arrived. This campaign was delayed however, with a new revolt breaking out in Egypt.

Xerxes began to assemble his army after about four years of preparation. Although the Greek historian Herodotus's estimation of the size of the Persian force was most likely exaggerated, (a figure of 200,000 is much more likely than the stated number of 2.5 million) the size of the Persian army was the largest force of its day.

Xerxes sent ambassadors to the Greek city-states demanding food, water, and land as evidence of their submission to his rule. These ambassadors, due to the previous experience with Sparta and Athens, decided to stay away from those two city-states, hoping to prevent them from being prepared for the coming invasion. This plan did not work, however, as other Greek poleis which were opposed to Xerxes rule over their city-states banded together to form an alliance against the Persian onslaught.

Although only about 10% of the roughly 700 different Greek city-states joined, this alliance would become a powerful foreshadowing of Greek unification. At this time, the Greek poleis were loosely affiliated with one another, if at all. Many of these city-states were even at war with one another. Not much is known about the inner-workings of this confederation, however it is known that among the alliance's powers was that of sending troops to a location after consulting the matter.

In 480 BC, a mere six years after his rise to power, Xerxes's army crossed over their pontoon bridges at Hellespont into Greece. The Greek alliance planned to send its troops to defend against Xerxes's advance at the Vale of Tempe, however this plan was abandoned with news of the tactical risks.

Themistocles, a great Athenian general, proposed a second plan. In order to reach the Southern part of Greece, Xerxes would have to funnel his forces through the narrow pass of Thermopylae (hot gateways.) Themistocles suggested that the larger Persian force could be stopped were the Greeks to send its hoplites to block the pass. In addition, the Greek ships would block the sea strait of Artemisium to ensure that the Persian forces couldn't sidestep the pass of Thermopylae by sea.

The plan had a hitch though, as the estimated arrival of the Persian forces to Thermopylae would coincide with not only the Olympic games, but also with the festival of Carneia. Carneia took place between August (the Greek month of Carneus) 7th and the 15th. This was a festival to honor Apollo Carneus, and was of particular importance to the Spartans. Due to the observance of this festival, and the perceived sacrilege implied by committing warfare during this period, the Spartan force consisted only of King Leonidas and his personal bodyguard of 300 men.

The usual hippeus (Spartan royal honor guard) consisted of young men, but as the destruction of his force was all but assured, the guard was replaced by men who had already fathered children. Along with the Spartan force of 301 men (Counting Leonidas,) there was a supporting army of the allies who joined the defense of Thermopylae. Additional forces were gathered along their way.

Upon their arrival at Thermopylae, the allied army rebuilt the Phocian wall at the tightest place in the pass. Xerxes waited for three days for the men to leave the pass. It wasn't until he was finally convinced that this small force intended to hold the hot gateways that Xerxes sent his men to attack.

Despite overwhelming numbers, the allies had a few key elements on their side. Due to the narrowness of the pass, the larger force of the Persian army was forced to meet the phalanx (a close, usually rectangular formation of soldiers) of the Greeks straight on, causing their men to fall quickly at the hands of the superior tactic of the allied army. Also, the Spartans, despite their smaller numbers, were exceptionally well-trained, as they were brought up from childhood to be soldiers. They also had, surprisingly enough, a great amount of morale due to the knowledge that they were choosing to fight (and die) by their own choice, and the invading force was one of slaves and conscripted men.

The allied forces held out against the massive Persian armies for a period of two days until a local man named Ephialtes betrayed them by disclosing a path behind the Greek forces to Xerxes. Leonidas caught wind of the betrayal, and released the larger part of the combined army, keeping only his men and a handful of other volunteers, leaving a grand total of about 2,000 men to cover the retreat of the rest of the forces. According to Herodotus, these men stood defiant against the prospect of certain destruction. Xerxes, not wanting to lose any more of his men, called upon his archers to deliver the final blow against the allied forces at Thermopylae.

Although this battle was lost, one crucial thing came of it. The Greeks began to see that unification could and would be to the benefit of the poleis, so long as these cities were allowed to keep their freedom.

While the battle of Thermopylae was taking place, another impressive battle was being carried out on the seas. Xerxes's navy was engaged in a naval battle against 271 allied Greek triremes. The Greeks were covering the flank of the army at Thermopylae. The allied navy held up against the Persian onslaught for the space of about three days until, hearing of the outcome of the battle at Thermopylae, the damaged allied vessels retreated as they were no longer needed.

After Thermopylae, Xerxes went on to conquer all of Boeotia, and subsequently most of Greece. Themistocles hatched a desperate plan. Before the first battle, he had consulted with the oracle at Delphi. The message from the Delphic oracle was as follows:

"Now your statues are standing and pouring sweat. They shiver with dread. The black blood drips from the highest rooftops. They have seen the necessity of evil. Get out, get out of my sanctum and drown your spirits in woe." (Fontenrose, 1981)

The message was a great blow to the Greeks, however, when consulted again, the oracle gave them a way out:

"A wall of wood alone shall be uncaptured, a boon to you and your children." (Fontenrose, 1981)

The city-state of Athens had no wooden walls at this time, but Themistocles took the second divination as the Greeks' way to victory. He believed that the wall of wood described a force of Greek Triremes, the most advanced ships in the armada. He commissioned hundreds of these ships to be made, and the beginning stages of his plan began to come together.

When Xerxes and his forces advanced toward Athens, Themistocles convinced them to do something drastic. The Athenians evacuated their homes and ultimately their city. Athens fell to the Persians, and their homes, temples, and most of the city was destroyed. Xerxes, frustrated at having received more resistance than he had hoped for, decided that his best bet in ending the conflict quickly was to destroy the Greek armada.

Led by Themistocles, the force of Greek triremes was stationed off the coast of Salamis, and Themistocles put his plan into action. He sent Xerxes a note disguised as a treasonous missive which told Xerxes of the armada's location. What he didn't convey was that the Greeks had hoped for Xerxes's armada to join battle with the Greek triremes in this place because, much like at Thermopylae, the superior Persian numbers would be forced to attack the Greeks in a narrow strait, thereby levelling the playing field.

The plan worked. According to Herodotus, Xerxes sat upon his throne on a beach, watching the naval battle commence. His fleet was torn apart by that of the Greeks, and the battle was lost. It's said that about 200 Persian ships were sunk or captured by the Greek navy, and the battle was a red-letter victory for the forces of Greece.

Xerxes, infuriated at the loss of his naval superiority fled back to his empire, leaving Mardonius, his brother-in-law to complete the subjugation and conquest of Greece. Although the war was not yet over, the Greeks would prevail against the Persian forces, and return to their homes after the battle of Salamis-in-Cyprus.

In 478 BC, The Delian League was formed to ally various poleis against the threat of Persia after the second invasion. Somewhere between 150 and 172 individual city-states came together to form the Delian league. This group got its modern name from their meeting place on the island of Delos. Athens grew rich and powerful through its influence in the league and, much to the chagrin of smaller, less powerful states, grew to a great deal of overall superiority. It wasn't long after the inception of the Delian League Athens took control of the league's navy, and the Athenian proclivity toward heavy-handed tactics for its own interest led to the Peloponnesian War. The league was disbanded at the conclusion of this war.

These years of conflict with the Persians had certainly taken their toll on Greece and its people, however, with victory came a new kind of unification among the Greek poleis, and gave rise to the golden age of Greece.

CHAPTER 5

Pericles and the Golden Age

Also called the classical age, the golden age of Greece lasted between about 480-300 BC. Although the Athenians and the Spartans came together to fight the Persians, they would remain rivals throughout most of their existence in the ancient times.

Much of the history that we have of Greece was recorded by a man named Herodotus (484-409 BC.) He was a historian, in fact, he's often known as the father of history (although Voltaire would later refer to him as the father of lies.) Herodotus was the first known historian to not only retell, or collect history, but to take certain measures to test the authenticity of the stories of the day and of the past.

The golden age of Greece was a veritable explosion of philosophy, art, and architecture. This period was home not only to Herodotus, but to philosophers such as Socrates, Plato, and Aristotle, men whose insights would not only change the thoughts of the day, but live on to affect us in modern times. We will get to them in the next chapter.

Discussion of the golden age of Greece cannot be in any way thorough without taking a look at Pericles. Pericles (495-429 BC) began taking part in politics in Athens around 472 BC. As son to a well-known politician, a man by the name of Xanthippus, Pericles was encouraged at a young age to become involved with politics and government.

Athens was still reeling from the impact of the wars with Persia, and it was a long and difficult process toward rebuilding and restoring order. Pericles saw the wealth that was accruing to Athens through the Delian League, and contrasted this with the fact that Athens had not been fully rebuilt. Rather than add to the force of the navy by manpower, or construction of triremes, many of the city-states in the Delian League elected instead to donate money and other provisions. With this wealth, the city of Athens was poised, not only for rebuilding, but for a large-scale glorification of their city.

Although, after continued campaigns by the Delian League against Persia had rendered the former foe inconsequential as a threat to the Greeks at the time, Pericles insisted that the other members of the dissolving council continue to donate as they had when military campaigns were at their height. Pericles eventually raided the stockpile of wealth at Delos and brought it to his home polis of Athens.

With this influx of wealth, Pericles had the city and its temples restored. Along with this, he commissioned the building of the Parthenon, a site which, although in ruins today, still holds a great deal of interest to Athens and indeed the world. The Parthenon housed an enormous statue of Athena, and was certainly an incomparable testament to the artistry and craftsmanship of the day. No expense was spared, and it is interesting to note that the Parthenon doesn't actually contain any right angles. It was built in such a way as to compensate for the illusion which is created by intersecting lines that makes them appear to bow.

It is often said, as Thucydides once remarked, that Athens during this time was only a democracy in its appearance, while in actuality, it was ruled by Pericles, sometimes known as The First Citizen of Athens.

With the outbreak of the Peloponnesian War, a conflict between Athens and its allies against Sparta and its allies which lasted approximately 30 years, not only would the supremacy of Athens come under fire, but the control of Athens by the Athenians was also culled.

The Peloponnesian war began when Athens made it apparent that Persia was not to fear, Athens was. The parties of the Delian League were taken advantage of by the Athenians and Sparta wasn't willing to trade one dictator abroad for one closer to home. The most complete account of the Peloponnesian war was made by General Thucydides, an aforementioned ally of Pericles.

Athens basically controlled the Delian League however Sparta, never to be outdone, had its own league called The Peloponnesian League. The Peloponnesian League was vast and powerful. When the helots, Sparta's slave class, revolted in 465 BC, Athens sent a force to support the Spartans, however their assistance was refused as Sparta believed the force was intended, not to aid Sparta, but to take advantage of the conflict.

In 449, two members of the Peloponnesian League came into conflict. Athens and Megara formed an alliance and decided to enter into the conflict. This resulted in Spartan forces pitting themselves against Athens, and is often referred to as the First Peloponnesian War. The outcome of this conflict ended in 445 BC with an agreement of peace between the two empires known as the 30 Years Peace. The terms set down basically came down to the Athenian Empire and the Spartan Empires agreeing to not get involved with matters of their respective groups.

The Athenians, however, did not long hold to this agreement and set about involving themselves in acts such as taking over settlements, imposing sanctions, and striking out against the Peloponnesian League at large. Under Pericles, a wall was built between Athens and its port of Piraeus so that Athens, even if besieged by Sparta, would be able to import whatever goods it required from its growing empire, and it would never have to meet the fierce Spartan army on its own terms. Due to Athenian naval superiority, it was able to move much more quickly than the Spartan army, and even bypass it entirely. For this purpose, much of the Spartan force was required to stay in and around Sparta for fear of an Athenian attack. Athens, Pericles theorized, would remain safe so long as it didn't attempt to expand its empire.

Unfortunately for Athens, the construction of this wall encased the citizens of the polis in close quarters, and in a relatively short amount of time, these close quarters along with a lack of general sanitation led to an outbreak of plague which killed an estimated 30,000 Athenian citizens. Pericles himself succumbed to this plague, and died within six months of contracting it.

With the death of Pericles, rule of the city went to various demagogues until Alcibiades took control of the polis. He went against the non-expansion which Pericles had insisted upon and sought to grow the Athenian Empire. Alcibiades led a campaign to take Sicily which was, at that time, under attack from Syracuse. Upon his return, however, Alcibiades went, not back to the Athenians, but to Sparta. His allegiance would switch many times between alliance to Athens and allegiance to Sparta, no doubt weakening the cause of Athens.

Alcibiades was eventually killed, not just for his ambivalent alliances to Greek States, but also at times with Persia. The Athenians were caught in a state of discord as many leaders would follow Alcibiades in their lust for control over the Athenian Empire. Multiple further campaigns were sent to Sicily, and all of them failed, eventually decimating the naval supremacy of Athens. This wouldn't be the last word on the Athenian navy, however, as they built new ships and formed new armies.

Things finally turned after the battle of Arginusae. Although the Athenian fleet had won a great battle, the brilliant naval commanders were executed due to their retreat from a storm in order to save their ships. Without the skilled leadership of these commanders, the Athenian Navy was eventually decimated by a Spartan fleet that sailed in Persian ships. The polis of Athens would eventually be starved into submission.

This Spartan victory led to the end of the war in 404 BC and the eventual subjugation of Athens by Sparta. A group known as the 30 tyrants who led Athens now, not in a democracy as it had been, but an oligarchy (rule by a small group of people.) This oligarchy would not stand however, as Athens was eventually able to retake their city and their democracy about a year after the institution of the 30 tyrants.

This war was costly to both sides, and eventually led to the fall of both poleis to outside forces.

In the north, a city called Macedon was not far from coming to a level of power as yet unknown in Greece, or indeed the world. Macedon had long battled against barbarian invaders, and had fallen into bad a rapport with the more influential city-states of the time. The Macedonians were often considered to be hardly civilized themselves, but it would be the successive reign of one man and his son that would change the political and cultural landscape of the world.

Philip II (382-336 BC) came to power in 359 BC. Philip had a vision for Macedon and for Greece itself. He wasted no time in getting his plans off the ground. The common practice of warfare in Greece at the time was based on the phalanx formation, and Philip's armies were no different in that fundamental aspect. However, it was the development of weaponry, diplomatic relations, and a change to a professional, well trained army that would make these plans possible.

Macedon had lost key battles before Philip II's accession to the throne. Philip was quick to forge alliances with neighboring cities and set about rebuilding the army. He not only rebuilt the army in numbers, but oversaw the development of a few different types of weapons that would make the Macedonian military the envy of the world. One of these weapons was called the sarissa.

The sarissa was a pike, or long spear, up to about 20 feet in length. Used in a phalanx and in conjunction with cavalry units, the sarissa could keep enemy forces at bay and at a distance while they were being flanked. Enemies had nothing to match the length of the sarissa, and were more often than not at the mercy of the Macedonian forces at the tips of these pikes.

Another important innovation was that of the gastraphetes (belly-shooters.) Unlike the traditional bow and arrow that only had as much force as the archer had strength in his arms, gastraphetes were crossbows which harnessed the power of a man's whole body. These weapons were a far sight more powerful and more effective against enemy units, especially in siege operations, than bows and arrows.

Along with sarissas and gastraphetes, two types of torsion ballistae were developed: oxybeles (bolt-shooters) and lithobolos (stone-shooters.) The oxybeles could fling a large bolt to lengths of up to a quarter mile, and easily penetrate enemy armor. The lithobolos could hurl stones up to 180 pounds in weight a great distance, effectively making the Macedonian forces unmatched in distance warfare.

One of Philip's sons, a young man who would grow to join his father on his military campaigns, and eventually become king was named Alexander. Alexander (more commonly referred to as Alexander the Great) came under the tutelage of Aristotle, a well-known and important philosopher at the age of 13.

When his father was battling against Byzantium, Alexander was left in charge. A group called the Maedi staged a revolt against Macedonia, and Alexander was put to an early test. He quickly drove the Maedi from their land and settled his own countrymen in their place and founded Alexandropolis, the first, but far from the last city that Alexander would name for himself.

By 346 BC, Philip's power had grown to a level which, in practice, set him as the leader of Greece. The Greek city-states resented the reach of Philip's power, and began to build their resistance to him. In 338 BC, allied Greek poleis, including Athens and Thebes, fought against Philip and Alexander in the battle of Chaeronea.

Alexander was only 18 at the time of the battle, and when he and his father prevailed against the forces of Athens and Thebes, Philip was in a position to destroy or rule these city-states in whatever way he so desired. In a gesture that was completely unexpected by these conquered city-states, Philip allowed the men to return to their homes and carry on within their cities as they had done before the conflict. Philip loved the culture of Greece, and wished for the territories he had conquered to retain their individuality.

Philip would die in 336 BC, just before mounting his ultimate plan of invading the vast and powerful empire of Persia, at the hands of one of his own bodyguards. During his 20 years ruling Macedon, Philip had made his once looked-down-upon city the seat of the Greek Empire. Alexander, now 20, would take the throne of Macedon.

Being only half-Macedonian himself and having a slew of relatives (Philip had seven wives, only one of which was Macedonian,) Alexander had rivals for the succession to his father's throne. His first order of duty was to remove the contentious parties, many of them by death.

Once secured as king, Alexander followed in his father's footsteps and set out to conquer Greek's long-time enemy of Persia. Before he set off to the east, he put down a number of rebellions, including that of Thebes and Athens.

With the seat of his power secure, Alexander set off for Persia. The Persian Empire stretched from the Middle East to parts of Asia and included portions of

Northern Africa, most notably Egypt. Alexander's task was an enormous one, but he showed his intentions famously by striking a spear into the ground in Asia and proclaimed that he accepted the land as a gift from the gods.

Alexander would win multitudinous victories, cutting his way through the Persian Empire, assaulting Persian cities and harbors, rendering Persian naval forces ineffectual. One of the most impressive victories on his way through the Persian Empire was at the battle of Tyre.

Tyre was a largely fortified city in the Mediterranean Sea that was proving to be difficult to take due to its distance from the shore. The port of Tyre was the last remaining harbor in the region still in his enemy's hands, and so Alexander wasn't about to abandon his campaign against the city.

He made a couple of offers to the Tyrians to avoid full-on conflict. One was that he would leave the people their lives if he was allowed to make a sacrifice at the temple of Melqart, as he equated Melqart with Heracles. He then sent representatives to discuss an agreement of peace, but they were killed and thrown from the city walls into the sea.

Alexander ordered that a siege be staged against the city, and he built a causeway, roughly 2/3 of a mile long (1 kilometer) to the Tyrian shore. With the use of siege towers, he eventually took the city and, frustrated by the stubbornness of the Tyrians, he set fire to the city.

Alexander continued his campaigns and before he was done, he was hailed as King of Macedonia (336-323 BC), Pharaoh of Egypt (332-323 BC), King of Asia (331-323 BC), and King of Persia (330-323 BC.)

Alexander died of an unknown illness in 323 BC. Accounts differ on some of the specifics, such as whether or not he had a fever. There were claims that he was poisoned, but these were largely discounted as he lived for nearly two weeks after taking ill. His military campaigns and his reign over much of the known world would become the stuff of legend.

The Classical Age of Greece effectively came to an end with Alexander's death.

Although this time period was often rife with conflict, it also produced many of the most fantastical wonders of the Greek world. Culture flourished, and many of the Athenian arts, architecture, and philosophies are still something to marvel at to this day.

CHAPTER 6

Philosophy and Discord

Socrates was often described as a plainly ugly man who travelled around wearing a single robe. He was born an Athenian in 469 BC, and would live until his sentence of death by hemlock was carried out in 399 BC. Despite his genius, Socrates was illiterate and therefore his words were collected by Plato and Xenophon, two of his students. Along with his incredible mind, Socrates was also known for his strength, and he fought in the Peloponnesian War.

Although Socrates was an incredibly astute man, when he was proclaimed by the Oracle of Delphi to be the wisest man in all of Athens, he was taken aback, and postulated that either all men must be equally ignorant, or that he was wise by his awareness of his ignorance. His penchant for getting lost in thought was the stuff of legend, and he is claimed to have gotten so wrapped up in his thoughts one day that he stood in one spot, unmoving for the entire length of that day.

His philosophy was one of free-thinking, and questioning the ideas presented through logical processes, each for himself or herself. The Socratic method was a practice of discussion and critical thinking that was intended to question even one's own thoughts and opinions and checking them for their plausibility. Elenchus (proving an idea false by showing its opposite to be true) was the predominant form of Socratic criticism.

In 399 BC, the tyrants of Athens were overthrown. Although Socrates had often shown himself to be a friend to the people of Athens, only suggesting that they look within and without themselves to challenge their beliefs, he was accused of poisoning the minds of the children. He was held for trial, and acted in his own defense. The "courts" of the time were much different than those with which we are familiar today. He was given a brief period in which to defend himself, and used this time to logically prove that he wasn't subject to trial and, in fact, should be honored with free food for the remainder of his life, and held as a benefactor of the people. The judges weren't pleased with his defense and found him guilty, sentencing him to death by hemlock. It was said by his student Xenophon that Socrates's defiance was intentional with the purpose to offend the judges and secure a guilty verdict. According to Xenophon, Socrates believed that he was better off dead.

Socrates was jailed for about a month, but was allowed visitors. The hemlock poison which Socrates was to drink caused an extremely painful death, however when his friends came to him before he drank the poison, he spent his time peacefully discussing the immortality of the soul. Socrates actually had a chance to escape the city, and thus, his sentence, as his friends successfully bribed a guard, but Socrates refused to leave. He reasoned that, even were his verdict to be unfair, it was more important to obey these laws even if it meant his death. Otherwise, the state would have come to harm by this flight from captivity. He willingly drank the hemlock potion dry.

It is postulated by some that Socrates was not in fact a real man, but a creation of Plato. The argument is that Plato formulated the great philosopher in order to give added weight to his own theories. Although there is still debate today about the actual existence of the man named Socrates, the fact remains that his philosophies, whether formulated by himself as a real man, or by Plato as a means to further his own career, have had an enormous impact not only in the time of his life, but throughout the ages, continuing to this day.

Plato (born somewhere between 428 and 423 BC, and died around 347 BC) was a great philosopher and student of Socrates, is quite possibly the most influential philosopher of all time. Plato's prolific written work was not purveyed in the manner to which we are commonly accustomed, but set down as a series of events which usually contained a debate between philosophers.

Plato's ideal government was one where enlightened philosophers would be elevated to the level of kings, as it was only the philosophers who could justly rule. Believing, as Socrates was purported to have said (paraphrased here), that a life without questioning one's beliefs is not a life worth living; it's no leap to understand why Plato favored this form of govern-ment, although it would never take form.

One of his predominant philosophies was that of The Theory of Forms. Although this philosophy is now widely discredited, it was often central to Platonic thought. The gist of this philosophy is that what we can perceive is not, in fact, the solid nature of things, but rather (as he would state in the cave analogy) that they are mere shadows *of* the purified forms which are invisible to us.

Plato also believed that knowledge isn't acquired, rather, it is *remembered*. Plato postulated that origi-nally, we had the full and complete knowledge of every aspect of existence, however, we would lose these things and any knowledge that we might gain throughout our lives was a mere remembrance of previously known things.

Although these are a few examples of Platonic thought, this is by no means intended to be a comprehensive list of Plato's philosophy.

A student of Plato, a philosopher by the name of Aristotle (384-322 BC), was regarded to be one of the well-versed philosophers, not only of the ancient world, but of all time. Although, as with many of the ancient philosophers, a large part of his philosophical theories have been discarded, he was and is a very influential man in the field of philosophy. Although a student of Plato, Aristotle rejected the Theory of Forms.

One of Aristotle's philosophies was that of incidental and essential features. For instance, a rock can be black, brown, red, or green and it is still a rock. This would be an example of an incidental feature. However, a rock's composition would be a necessary feature, as a rock made out of feathers would not, in actuality, be a rock.

Aristotle developed a method called formal logic which is still widely used today. The use of formal logic can be illustrated by use of syllogism. This method postulates that new knowledge can be deduced by the combination of previously verified truths. An example would be: All men are six feet tall. John is a man. If John is a man, then he is six feet tall. In this example is also illustrated a further part of formal logic which is that if one of the two propositions is found to be untrue, then the conclusion cannot be said to be necessarily true itself. In this case, it's not true that all men are six feet tall, therefore it can only be deduced from this information that some men may be six-feet tall, but men (including John) aren't necessarily of this height.

Aristotle also believed that any statement could only be true or false. The problem with this philosophy, however, arises when postulating future-oriented statements. If one person says that they were going to walk to the store and randomly meet a tall woman named Daphne and another person said that he would not meet such a woman, but a short man named Bruce then which one of them was telling the truth? Before the event, this is unknowable. Another problem arises if, when arriving at the store, the first person actually does meet a short man named Bruce, this person can't argue that the other was wrong in their statement, even though the result happened out of mere happenstance.

These are but a few examples of a few of the theories of a few of the philosophers of the day. Philosophy during this time was highly revered, and these men (and many others) made an indelible mark on the world with their ideas.

CHAPTER 7

Enter the Roman Empire

Greek sovereignty was not to last forever. Many invaders entered and conquered various states of Greece; however the Roman conquest of Greece would prove the largest empirical change to the region for many years to come.

The Punic wars lasted from 264 to 146 BC and were predominantly a conflict between Rome in modern day Italy and Carthage in northern Africa. Although, during the Third Punic War, the conflict wasn't contained in the land-mass of Greece, the Romans had become increasingly irritated by the agitation of the Greek states.

The growing Roman power had fought many battles within the land of Greece; however, it was the Roman conquest of the city of Corinth that brought things to a head. The Romans fought against the Corinthians and their allies of the second Achaean League, a confederation of Greek city-states in the north-central area of Peloponnese.

The Romans, well known as fierce expansionists, finally took the City of Corinth in 146 BC, and although this was not the immediate end of the Greek empire, it was the first major blow toward this end. Although the Achaean League revolted against its Roman invaders, the onslaught of the Romans was only beginning.

Not only were cities taken, but the Greek religion was absorbed and equated with that of the Romans. Deities such as Zeus, Aphrodite, and Ares were equated with Jupiter, Venus, and Mars respectively. This cultural shift played a big part in the Romanization of the Greek empire.

The Greek Peninsula at large would come under the control of Rome or its prefecture in 146 BC with the Aegean Islands following suit in 133 BC. Greece had long been influential in Roman life and culture. Under the rule of Rome, Greek culture was actually much the same as it had been. This continuity of Greek culture lasted until the arrival of Christianity, even though Greek independence was ended.

Greece and Rome were long intertwined, not necessarily as allied forces, but as a sharing of cultures. This is by no means to suggest that these cultures didn't clash with each other, although there was often a level of give-and-take on this cultural level.

CONCLUSION

We have arrived at the conclusion of this book. I want to thank you for joining me on this incredible journey through one of the greatest civilizations that our world has ever seen.

History, even ancient history such as this, is important, not only because it tells us where we came from and what affected the world of the past, but it has shaped all of us, Greek or no in our societies and our cultures.

From the philosophers such as Socrates, Plato, and Aristotle to the military leaders such as Thucydides, Leonidas, and Philip II, the times and places associated with Ancient Greece have left their indelible imprint on our world, and indeed, on all of us who live in it.

With history, we find myth and fact, truth and legend about the people who lived during these far away times. We also find in our own civilizations today marks of those seemingly distant times. By looking at the past, we can better understand our present, and plan for a better future with the lessons long ago learned, passed down through countless generations of men and women whose own lives form a lineage, a direct connection with those times.

It has been an absolute pleasure to delve into this elegant, often troubled time in the history of the world and share with you a collection of some of the events that took place to shape an incredible empire.

From its humble beginnings to the unprecedented reign of Alexander the Great, Greece has been a fascination of millions of people throughout the ages. I hope that you have enjoyed this journey as much as I have, and I hope that you'll press on with the other histories in this series to discover even more about the civilizations that have set the stage for our modern life.

When we look back into the past, we see ourselves in the cacophony of the times which have preceded our own. Peace and war, enlightenment and ignorance, and the individual journeys of the heroic and the common alike no doubt will continue to shape our world as we move forward, day by day, in our own quests for greatness.

Thank you,

Martin R. Phillips

PART **2**
GREEK MYTHOLOGY

Discovering Greek Mythology

INTRODUCTION

I want to thank you and congratulate you for downloading the book, Greek Mythology.

One of the most interesting aspects of the ancient Greeks is their mythology. Although only a small handful of people still believe the myths to be true, what remains is that Greek mythology fascinates us in a way that is almost incomparable to other ancient systems of belief.

Culture has yet to turn away from the mythology of the ancient Greeks, and this fact can be seen in various aspects of our modern life. Through various forms of entertain-ment, we come across themes and events depicted in Homer's works of the Iliad and Odyssey. We find ourselves viewing and referencing the strength and trials of Heracles. We even find various parallels between the lives and myths of the ancient Greeks to our own modern world.

The history of Greece herself cannot be separated by the mythology of its ancient peoples. From heroes such as Heracles and Perseus, to the underhanded dealings of gods and mortals alike, their story is one a creative attempt to understand the forces which dwell about us and within us.

In this book you will find specific stories central to Greek mythology. This is a key into understanding the mindset, not only of these ancient peoples, but of our modern world as well. We may not subscribe as the Greeks did to these myths as factual accounts of historical events, however, these tales allegorically represent the things that humankind still endures and rejoices in.

In this text, you will find the spirit of love, of nature, of war and of peace. These myths often deal with very blunt subject matter, as they were the dominant lens through which the world was viewed during much of ancient Greece.

The research and writing involved in bringing you this collection of Greek mythology has been an absolute pleasure, and I hope that you are as fascinated in reading this as I was in putting it together.

Thanks again, I hope you enjoy it!

CHAPTER **8**

In the Beginning, There was Chaos

In this chapter, we will be discussing the origin of the universe according to Greek mythology and the generations of the primordial gods, the Titans, and the Olympians.

According to Greek mythology, the universe began as an abyss. There was no matter, no light, no life or consciousness outside of this primordial chasm. Yet it was out of this very void, known as Chaos (or Khaos) that not only the Titans and later the gods of Olympus were sprung, but existence itself.

It was from Chaos that Gaia (or Gaea, "mother earth") was formed. Along with Gaia, Tartarus (the abyss, often described as a vast cave-like space beneath the earth, comparable to hell in Judeo-Christian belief), Eros (desire/biological imperative; some myths include him as a primordial god, while others claim him as a child of Aphrodite) Erebus (darkness) and Nyx (the night) were also spawned of Chaos. While other beings that would represent other necessary factors for life as we know it were later formed by Gaia and her ilk, the initial building blocks of reality were spawned directly from Chaos.

The Chaos mythos in ancient Greek religion is an interesting one. Although the myths were around long before them, two poets were the earliest sources of known, written accounts dealing with the religion of ancient Greece. Those two men were Homer and Hesiod.

Homer is best known for his two epics Iliad and Odyssey which deal largely with the Trojan wars; wars that up until more recently were considered to be a complete fabrication. It's not within the scope of this book to delve too deeply into the purported Trojan wars themselves outside of the later chapter regarding Homer's works; however, reference to these epics form much of the basis of our understanding of Greek mythological belief.

Hesiod is also best known for two epic poems, Theogony and Works and Days. It is with Theogony that this text is primarily concerned, as it delves into the mythological creation and formation of all that exists, along with the Olympian gods, their progenitors and progenies.

At the earliest times within the Greek creation myth, there was, as yet, no male presence. Gaia took it upon herself to rectify this by birthing Uranus. Gaia produced other children asexually, they were: Ourea (mountains) and Pontus (sea). Thus completes the basic structure of the planet as the Greeks would view it.

Gaia bore many other children however. With her son Uranus, she bore the Hecatonchires (indomitable giants with a hundred hands), the Titans (a powerful race of deities with whom the next chapter is primarily concerned), the Cyclopes (more commonly Cyclops; one-eyed giants) and Echidna (often known as the mother of all monsters).

With Tartarus, she conceived and gave birth to her final son Typhon. Typhon was a dragon with a hundred heads, considered the most deadly of all monsters, and in some traditions, considered the father of all monsters.

Other primordial gods produced their own offspring which covered much of life's experience. Erebus and Nyx generated Aether (the heavens, also the air which the gods breathed) and Hemera (day). On her own, Nyx generated many descendants. These were Apate (deception), Eris (discord), Geras (maturation, or aging), Hypnos (sleep), the Keres (eaters of the dead or wounded on the battlefield), the Moirai (the fates), Momus (blame or denunciation), Moros (doom), Nemesis (revenge or retribution), Oizys (suffering), Oneiroi (Dreams), Philotes (affection) and Thanatos (death).

Uranus also produced his own children, although this was not by choice. His children were purportedly spawned when Cronos {one of the principle Titans} castrated Uranus. The blood that had spilled would go on to create the Erinyes (the furies, female deities of vengeance), the Giants (aggressive and strong beings, although not necessarily larger than human), the Meliae (ash tree nymphs). Also, when the severed genitals of Uranus washed ashore, Aphrodite (the goddess of love among other things) came into being among the sea foam.

While there are many other gods in the Greek pantheon, the present list is intended to show the first few emanations of Greek deities from Chaos to Aphrodite. Other gods, their children, consorts, etc. will be referenced in later chapters.

It is interesting to note that while Greek mythology was unique in many ways, there are common threads throughout many of the world's religions. For instance, in the belief of Judaism and its descendants Christianity and Islam, at the time of creation, the world was without form and [was] void. The formation came through god's will. Although these religions are monotheistic (belief in one god) as opposed to the polytheistic (belief in multiple gods) religion of the ancient Greeks, the story of creation has its similarities. The primary difference being that where the Greeks saw many emanations of gods that created existence, in the monotheistic religion, this was carried out by one god alone.

Other religions with similarities are the Babylonian where the earth began as a dark, watery chaos; the Hindu cosmology, the universe began as empty and dark. Even Norse mythology has its origin story begin in chaos.

It is hardly difficult to realize that in order to have an account of creation, there has to be something before creation. Even the scientific theory of the big bang has the universe composed with all matter in an infinitely small point; outside of this was nothingness (which could be called chaos).

CHAPTER 9

The Titans' Rule

The story of the rise of the Titans begins with the god of the sky, Uranus. Uranus (the sky) and Gaia (the earth) were spouses, lovers and, together, parented the Hecatonchires, the Cyclopes, the Echidna and the Titans.

Uranus and Gaia's love affair was the stuff of legend (forgive the pun.) Uranus so loved Gaia that at night, he embraced her on all sides, mating with her. He was a devoted spouse, but was obsessed with power.

While Uranus was affectionate toward Gaia, and favored those that he would come to call Titans, he feared and despised the Hecatonchires, the Giants and the Cyclopes. He imprisoned them all in Tartarus, deep within Gaia.

The imprisonment of her children caused Gaia great pain emotionally and physically. In order to reap vengeance on her consort Uranus for what he had done to her and her children, Gaia fashioned a sickle made of flint and approached her Titan children for help. The plan was to castrate Uranus.

None of the Titans were willing to risk a confrontation with Uranus with the exception of the youngest and the most ambitious Titan. His name was Cronus.

Cronus took the sickle and laid in wait for his father to arrive. When Uranus came, Cronus ambushed him and succeeded in castrating him. Cronus cast the severed genitals into the sea, the blood of which would create the giants, the meliae and the erinyes. When the genitals washed up to shore, Aphrodite was created.

Uranus cursed his children and called them Titanes theoi, or "straining gods." There are differing legends on what happened to the sickle at this point. Some claimed that the sickle was buried in Sicily. Others would claim that the sickle had been cast into the sea. One Greek historian claimed to have found the sickle at Corcyra.

With Uranus out of the picture as ruler, Cronus came to power. Although his mother Gaia had intended for her other children, the Cyclopes and the hundred-handed ones to be released from their captivity, Cronus left them prisoners inside Tartarus. Along with them, he also imprisoned the giants. Having now angered both of his parents, Gaia and Uranus prophesied that Cronus would be himself overthrown by one of his children.

Cronus had married his sister Rhea and, fearing the prophecy of the earth and the sky, he took upon himself a desperate plan to preserve his power. When Rhea began to bear children, Cronus immediately devoured them. Although his children were immortal like him, they would, in their turn, be imprisoned within his belly.

Each of his children, the first of those who would come to be the gods of Olympus, were devoured by Cronus in this manner with the exception of the youngest child. Rhea was fed up with Cronus's actions and when she was about to bear her sixth and final child, she hid away and, once her child was born, she hid him in a cave on Mount Ida in Crete. This child's name was Zeus.

Knowing that Cronus would insist upon devouring the child, Rhea took a stone and wrapped it in swaddling clothes. Cronus devoured the stone, thinking it to be his child.

Despite Cronus's treatment of his children, the time during the rule of Cronus and Rhea was referred to as The Golden Age of the Gods. The earth was devoid of immorality. The inhabitants of the earth were moral on their own, and so did not require laws to keep them in line. This was before the existence of humankind.

There are different myths as to how Zeus was raised. One has him being raised by Gaia herself. Another has him being raised by a nymph named Adamanthea who, in order to protect the child, suspended him from a tree between the sky, the sea, and the earth, therefore keeping him just outside his father's kingdom and therefore outside of his perception. Another myth has Zeus being raised by a shepherd family in exchange for the protection of their flocks. In another telling, he was raised by a different nymph named Cynosura. In this myth, Zeus's gratitude would lead him to place Cynosura among the stars.

Yet another, and one of the more popular myths of the time, has Zeus being raised by a goat. His cries are said to have been covered by a group of armored dancers who would bang their shields together, shout and clap in order to mask the child's cries, thus keeping him outside the knowledge of Cronus.

Regardless the differing myths associated with his infancy, Zeus grew to become very powerful. When he reached manhood, he was set on overthrowing his father Cronus, and releasing his siblings from within the ruler's body. He met with Metis, a Titan of deep knowledge and wisdom. She gave him an emetic (a substance which causes one to purge) potion to give to his father.

According to one myth, Zeus slipped the concoction into Cronus's nightly drink of mead. Upon drinking the mixture, Cronus began to grow violently ill. He first vomited up the stone which he had thought to be Zeus, and then the children whom he had eaten. These children of Cronus and Rhea were quick to ally themselves with Zeus. They were Demeter, Hades, Hera, Hestia and Poseidon.

What followed is often referred to as the Titanomachy or War of the Titans. This conflict between the Titans on Mount Othrys, and the children of Cronus from Mount Olympus would last for ten years. Zeus, in search of more allies against the Titans travelled deep into Gaia to Tartarus and freed the Hecatonchires, the Giants and the Cyclopes. In gratitude for their release, the Cyclopes forged thunder and lightning and gave them to Zeus.

The Olympians would face nearly all of the Titans in this war with the exception of Themis and her son Prometheus; these two allied themselves with Zeus.

With his new allies and powers, the Olympians would defeat the Titans. Upon victory, Zeus imprisoned the Titans in Tartarus as Uranus and Cronus had imprisoned the Hecatonchires and the Cyclopes.

Zeus forced Atlas, one of the leaders of the Titan army, to hold up Uranus at the western edge of Gaia by his shoulders in order to prevent the mating of the two, and the possibility of further Titan births. It's commonly thought that Atlas was forced to hold up the earth, and is often pictured as supporting the globe on his back. However, this is a more modern interpretation, and the actual myth was that of separating Uranus and Gaia.

The Titan rule had come to an end, and the rule of Olympus had started.

CHAPTER 10

The Olympian Rule

Although which gods are included in the list of twelve Olympians varies, this number would be a constant of the major inhabitants of Olympus. Here it becomes useful to give an account of the major Olympian gods, their importance and their attributions. As the various consorts of these deities could fill up a book on their own, they will only be referenced in cases of particular importance.

Aphrodite was, as stated above, born from the sea foam after Cronus's genitals were cast into the sea. She was the goddess of love and beauty. She was among the gods invited to the wedding of Peleus and Thetis who would become the parents of the legendary Achilles. It was said that the only goddess not to be invited to the wedding was Eris, the goddess of discord.

When Eris showed up anyway, true to her nature, she tossed a golden apple into the center of the other goddesses inscribed with the words, "to the fairest."

Three of the goddesses immediately claimed that the gift was theirs by right of their beauty. These were Aphrodite, Hera and Athena.

When the three could not come to a decision regarding ownership of the golden apple, each thinking themselves to be the fairest of the goddesses, they brought the matter before Zeus. Wanting to avoid the quarrel, Zeus passed the decision onto Paris of Troy.

Paris was the son of the Trojan King Priam. The goddesses washed themselves in the spring of Mount Ida and went before Paris for his decision. They rent their clothing and asked him to judge. Although having been given permission to set his own conditions by Zeus, he could not decide among them as he found them all to be supremely beautiful.

The goddesses, undaunted by his inability to decide between them began offering him various things in exchange for his declaration of who was the fairest. Athena offered him wisdom, courage, and glory in battle; Hera offered control of Europe and Asia; but it was Aphrodite whose offer he accepted. Her offer was to grant him a wife who was more beautiful than all of the women of the earth.

The problem with Aphrodite's offer was that this woman was already married to a Spartan king named Menelaus. Undaunted, Paris abducted his new goddess-given bride, a woman named Helen out from under Menelaus. The legend goes that the other two goddesses, scorned Aphrodite and Paris for this, and they would go on to initiate the Trojan War, of which Homer's Iliad is largely concerned.

Apollo was the god of the sun, of light, of truth, and poetry among other things. He was often depicted as bearing a bow and arrow, or often a lyre. He was the son of Zeus and Leto, a daughter of Coeus and Phoebe (Titans), and twin brother to Artemis. Due to Hera's anger and jealousy of Leto as her husband had lain with her and the two produced offspring, Apollo's early life was largely occupied by protecting his mother against Hera's wrath.

Hera's first attempt on Leto was by sending Python, a dragon who dwelled beneath the living surface of Gaia. In order to be equipped to protect his mother, Apollo entreated Hephaestus to provide him with armaments. He received his iconic bow and arrow and, at only four days old, Apollo was said to have slain Python.

Hera wasn't done going after Leto, however. Her next attempt on Leto was commenced by sending the giant Tityos to dispatch her rival. Tityos was around twenty two square miles' worth of giant but, with the help of his sister Artemis, Tityos was defeated and cast into Tartarus by Zeus. While in Tartarus, Tityos was doomed to have his liver perpetually consumed by vultures.

Although he was considered a healer of man and god in Greek mythology, he also could bring death and disease with his arrows. One notable instance of this began with a simple insult.

Niobe was the wife of Amphion, one of the founders of Thebes and its ruler. She boasted to Leto that she had seven times as many children (seven sons and seven daughters) as Leto's two: Apollo and Artemis. Apollo and Artemis swiftly killed all (or in some versions, all but one) of Niobe's children; Apollo killed the sons while Artemis killed the daughters.

Apollo was bisexual and had a vast number of male and female consorts. He bore many children, however er the story of Apollo and Daphne is one of the most famous. As the story goes, Apollo was remarking to Eros that his bow and arrow were above his station, that he was unfit to wield them.

Eros, having had enough of Apollo's taunts shot two arrows: A golden arrow of love through Apollo's heart and a leaden arrow of hate or disgust into the nymph Daphne. Apollo immediately pursued the nymph who was disgusted and fled his advances. She entreated her father Peneus, the river god to help her. Her father turned her into a laurel tree, but Apollo's love of her was unwavering. He embraced the branches, but even they shrank away from him. He declared that as he retained eternal youth, so should the leaves of the tree never decay. He would guard the tree from any who would do it harm, and use its branches as crowns for the leaders of the world.

Ares was the god of war. A son of Zeus and Hera (one of Zeus's rare dalliances with his own wife), Ares took his sister Enyo (goddess of destruction) as his consort. He was the father of Phobos (fear) and Deimos (terror) borne from Aphrodite. According to Homer, Ares was despised by his father Zeus for his lust for war.

While he was immortal, and loved nothing more than warfare, he was highly intolerant of pain. In Homer's Iliad, Ares was injured in the battlefield of Troy, and his cries were heard throughout the world. He went back to Olympus whining to his father Zeus to heal him. Zeus quickly let Ares know how much he was despised but, as Ares was his son, he did in fact heal him.

Ares is said to have always gone into war with Enyo joining him on his chariot, and this chariot was driven by Phobos and Deimos.

Artemis, twin of Apollo, was the goddess of the hunt, the moon, the forests and the hills. She was the first of the twins to be born, and actually acted as midwife to her mother Leto during Apollo's birth. Her weapon was, like that of her brother, the bow.

Artemis believed her destiny to be as a midwife, and unlike many of the philandering gods, she remained a virgin. All of her companions were also virgins and, one day as they were bathing, a man named Actaeon came upon them. He was hunting with his hounds at the time, but was struck by the beauty of Artemis and her cohorts and stopped to gaze upon them further.

When Artemis discovered the man peeping at herself and her companions, she became furious and turned him into a stag. His hunting dogs, no longer recognizing their master tore him to pieces.

Artemis was certainly not one to be trifled with. When Agamemnon, one of the legendary warriors of the Trojan War in Iliad, offended Artemis, she exacted her vengeance by calming the winds which bore Agamemnon's fleet toward Troy. Stranded in the middle of the sea, Agamemnon's only choice to appease Artemis was to offer up his daughter Iphigenia.

There are differing accounts as to what exactly happened when Artemis came upon Iphigenia. Some myths say that Artemis spared the woman because of her bravery, others say that Iphigenia was taken as a priestess to help worshippers offer sacrifice to the goddess, while still others say that Athena did in fact take Iphigenia as sacrifice.

Athena was the goddess of wisdom, intelligence, crafts, and architecture and was the patron goddess of Athens which bears her name. Athena's birth is as interesting as any other myths about her. She was borne of the goddess Metis.

Metis was the goddess of wisdom and craftiness. Zeus and Metis became entangled in a romantic tryst but, fearing a prophecy which stated that Zeus's offspring by Metis would come to be more powerful than Zeus himself, he consumed Metis (in some versions, he turned her into a fly first) as his father Cronus had done with his Olympian children.

His efforts were too late, however, as Metis was already pregnant with Athena. Metis would give birth in Zeus's belly, and she forged weapons and armor for her new daughter. Athena grew to adulthood and split the head of Zeus, springing forth from within armed and grown. Zeus, despite the manner of Athena's technical birth, came through the encounter unscathed.

Other traditions do exist where Athena was born as the mind of god. She still sprung from his forehead, but as a result of his intention of creating another world by use of the word logos.

Among her other attributions was that she was a patron of heroes. In Homer's Odyssey, she is impressed by the hero Odysseus as he tries to make his way toward his home of Ithaca. She could only assist him from afar, however, by implanting thoughts into his head on his travel back to his homeland.

Demeter was the goddess of the harvest. Of all the cults in ancient Greece, the cults of Demeter were possibly the most widespread and definitely the most secretive.

As the story of Demeter and Persephone is detailed in the book Ancient Greece of this series, it seems fitting to give a different account of the goddess's myth.

During her search for Persephone, Demeter took the form of an elderly mortal woman and called herself Doso. She was found by four daughters of the king of Eleusis, a man named Celeus. She claimed that she had been attacked by pirates, and entreated them to help her find work befitting an old woman.

Demeter asked the king for shelter, which he gave. He asked if she could nurse his children Triptolemus and Demophon. Demeter did the king one better. Due to his kindness and hospitality, she secretly began feeding Demophon ambrosia (the food of the gods), a substance which would grant immortality to those who partook of it. Then at night, she would hold the boy in the fire to cleanse him of his mortality.

When the queen of Eleusis, Celeus's wife Metanira stumbled across the scene, she took the situation at face value and screamed. Demeter abandoned her quest to make the boy immortal, and instead taught his brother the secrets of planting, harvesting and agriculture. This is, according to Greek mythology, how the people of the earth learned to grow crops.

Dionysus was the god of wine and merriment. He was born of a mortal woman named Semele. Hera, usually quick to discover her husband's infidelities, went to Semele as a nurse, or an old woman. Semele told the disguised goddess of the unborn child's father, that it was Zeus's child.

Hera encouraged Semele to doubt the Olympian heritage of her unborn child. Semele then went before the disguised Zeus and demanded that he reveal himself. When she persisted, he reluctantly agreed and showed himself in all of his glory. As an unconcealed god, the mortal woman could not survive the sight, and she died in flame.

Zeus, not wanting his child to also perish, removed the still developing child Dionysus from his dead mother's womb. To allow the boy to grow to full infancy, Zeus sewed Dionysus into his thigh. After a few months of incubation, Dionysus was born. Thus, he was a twice-born god, once of his mother Semele and once from the thigh of Zeus himself.

In another popular Dionysian tale, Silenus, Dionysus's foster father had passed out in the rose garden of a king. The king nursed him back to health for ten days. On the eleventh day, Silenus took the king to Dionysus who, being so grateful for Silenus's return and the hospitality of the king, offered the latter his choice of any reward that he so chose.

The king's name was Midas.

Hades was the god of the underworld. Despite modern depictions, Hades was not the most reviled of all the gods. In fact, during the Titanomachy, he fought bravely with the Olympians against their Titan foes. He was the oldest male childe of Cronus and Rhea and was therefore the last to be regurgitated by the former. This being the case, he can also technically be considered the youngest male (Hestia being the oldest {and youngest} of all the children).

While there was a later belief that Hades and Dionysus were one and the same, the people feared Hades. They would sacrifice black animals such as sheep to the underworld god and, as it was believed that the blood dripped through a crack in the earth, would avert their faces to avoid seeing him.

Hades took Persephone as his wife, but when Demeter refused to allow the crops of the earth to grow, she was returned for two-thirds of the year.

His chariot was led by four black horses, and he kept as a pet and guardian the three headed dog Cerberus.

Hephaestus, the god of fire, masonry and metal working, was the only one of the gods who was considered to be ugly. Born of Zeus and Hera, he often took his mother's side. In a particular argument of the espoused gods, Hephaestus stepped in between them. Zeus, furious at Hephaestus's intervention cast him out of Olympus, throwing him by the leg.

Hephaestus flew for the space of a full day, finally landing with an enormous impact on the island of Lemnos. He was nursed back to health, but would always walk with a limp. (although another version has Hera casting him out because he already had a withered foot.)

Despite being cast out, Hephaestus was able to regain his place on Olympus.

In order to prevent the other gods from fighting over who would be able to marry Aphrodite, Zeus arranged the marriage between the goddess of beauty and Hephaestus. Although he was considered to be the most balanced of the gods, the insatiable Aphrodite was constantly unfaithful.

Although she was married to Hephaestus, Aphrodite had a long-running romance with Ares. The two were spotted one day by Helios (the charioteer of the sun), who quickly made Hephaestus aware of the situation.

Rather than confront them outright, Hephaestus set a trap. He forged a net which was so fine it could not be seen by the naked eye. He set his trap and waited for its prey.

When Ares and Aphrodite were ensnared, Hephaestus brought forth the two naked gods to shame them before the others on Olympus. The other gods, however, only laughed at the sight. It wasn't until Poseidon persuaded Hephaestus to release the two by promising that Ares would pay the fine of the adulterer, that of returning the wife and reclaiming the price he had paid as dowry to Zeus.

Aphrodite not only laid with Hephaestus's brother Ares, but a prodigious string of gods and men. Hephaestus was hardly a pitiable cuckold though, as he fathered many children and had many consorts of his own.

Hephaestus worked the forges both on Olympus, and within the volcanos of the earth. To help him walk, he forged two robots out of metal (not joking) and endowed them with the gift of artificial intelligence. These two robots would serve as highly intelligent crutches to the god.

Hera was the queen of the Olympian gods, and goddess of marriage, birth and women. Her symbol was the peacock, and these birds were said to have drawn her chariot.

Much of the stories regarding Hera are in regard to her vengeance upon the women with whom her husband Zeus engaged in sexual intercourse, and her wrath against the children born of these affairs.

One of the most amusing stories about Hera and her infamous temper regards a man named Tiresias. When he was young, he came across the sight of two mating snakes, and struck them with a stick. His intervention caused a strange consequence though, as he was changed into a woman.

During his nine years as a female, he married and bore children. He also became a priestess of Hera. When he came across another instance of two snakes mating, he again struck them with a stick and returned to his original male form.

In what can only be called an Olympian parlor bet, Zeus and Hera confronted Tiresias, asking him for whom sex was more pleasurable, men or women. The two gods believed that it was the sex opposite of theirs who enjoyed the greater ecstasy. Tiresias answered that sexual intercourse was more pleasurable for women. Enraged at the answer, Tiresias was struck blind by Hera.

Zeus could not restore Tiresias's sight; however, he did give him the gift of prophetic sight.

Hermes was the messenger of the gods. He was the son of Zeus and Maia. Among his other attributions, he was also the god of thieves, trade, athletes. He also guided souls to the underworld.

Hermes was a notorious trickster. While still an infant, he leapt from his cradle and hid Apollo's cattle. Apollo realized what was happening and confronted the child. Hermes insisted that he had nothing to do with it, so Apollo brought him before Zeus in a rage. Zeus, however, thought the matter was hilarious.

Like many of the other Olympians, Hermes was quite the philanderer. He never married, but fathered many children with over forty different women and goddesses.

He was also a patron to inventors, and is said to have invented music, numbers, the alphabet, astronomy, measurement, and many other indispensable creations.

Hestia was the goddess of architecture, the hearth and home, domesticity and the family. She was a daughter of Cronus and Rhea. She was a passive goddess, and is not always considered to be one of the twelve. In other myths, Dionysus replaces her on Olympus.

She remained a virgin, despite the advances of Apollo and Poseidon. She was directed by Zeus to tend the

Olympian fires. With any sacrifice, as Hestia was the oldest child of Cronus and Rhea (and the last to be purged, therefore also the youngest), Hestia was the first goddess to receive an offering.

Persephone was the daughter of Demeter and Zeus, and consort of Hades. Thus she was the goddess of the underworld. She is identified with the growth and productivity of the seasons, due to the above mentioned abduction and residence with Hades during what are the winter months.

Every spring as she returned from the underworld, the plant life would spring back up. As she was symbolically reborn, so were crops and other plants which had lain dormant in during her time in the underworld.

Poseidon was the god of the seas, earthquakes, storms, etc. His weapon (and symbol) was the trident. Another bisexual god, Poseidon had many consorts and children. He was often referred to as the earth shaker, and was one of the Olympian gods who fought against the Titans.

He was in competition against Athena to be the patron god of Athens. Although he lost the contest, he would remain a chief deity among the Athenians.

In Homer's Odyssey, he was angry with Odysseus (or Ulysses in Latin) for blinding one of his children, a

Cyclops. The god of the sea was infuriated, and set about making Odysseus's journey as difficult as possible. He, in fact, tried to kill Odysseus on more than one occasion, but was always thwarted.

Although much has already been covered in regard to Zeus (and much more will be covered) it seems fitting to give some information about the god outside of his poisoning his father Cronus, and his various infidelities.

Although the primary focus thus far has been on Zeus's various indiscretions (an accounting of his romantic endeavors alone would fill a few volumes), Zeus also had a protective side, especially toward Hera.

Ixion, king of the Lapiths in Thessaly, would come across Zeus in a way which was new to mortals of the time. According to myth, Ixion had married the daughter of Eioneus, but didn't pay the dowry. Eioneus, in order to have some assurance that Ixion would come to pay him, held his son-in-law's horses as collateral to ensure that payment would be made.

Ixion, however, was not about to give his new father-in-law his just dues. He lured Eioneus to his home, saying that he was ready to pay up, but killed Eioneus by casting into a flaming pit.

Killing a member of one's own family, in the myth, was unheard of, and those who could purify him refused to do so. Zeus, taking pity on the mortal invited Ixion to his table at Olympus, but Ixion's treachery was not over.

Ixion became enamored with, and began to pursue Hera. When Hera told Zeus about this, the king of the gods could hardly believe that one, especially someone in Ixion's position, would be so impudent as to make a move on his wife.

Zeus, as a test, created a cloud in the form of Hera (who would come to be called Nephele) and placed it in Ixion's bed (other stories have the cloud-Hera being placed in Hera's bed). Ixion had imbibed a few drinks at this point, and when he came across Nephele, he set himself upon it.

Zeus came in and, unable to deny Ixion's motives any longer, cast Ixion from Olympus, striking him with a thunderbolt. Ixion was bound to a flaming wheel, which was set to spin for eternity.

According to the myth, Nephele (cloud-Hera) had become pregnant through the dalliance with Ixion and gave birth to Centauros. Centauros would go on to mate with the horses of Mount Pelion, thus creating the race of Centaurs.

These are but a few stories related to the gods. The myths surrounding most of them are quite vast, and their essences are still about us today in popular and underground culture.

CHAPTER 11

Heracles and the Twelve Labors

Zeus (as is well established by now) was quite the playboy. How he ever got anything done between his affairs is astounding. However, one of his many children would come to be known as the divine hero. Quite possibly the most famous of Zeus's mortal children would be the one known as Heracles.

Heracles (the original figure from whom Hercules was adapted) was the son of Zeus and Alcmene. Zeus disguised himself as Alcmene's husband, Amphitryon, returning from the war of the time. He lied with her and swiftly departed. Later on that same evening, the real Amphitryon returned home. His wife, already impregnated by Zeus with Heracles, became pregnant that same night with the child of Amphitryon.

The hatred of Hera toward Heracles is legendary. This began its manifestation during Alcmene's pregnancy. Hera convinced Zeus to declare that the next high king would be of the house (a descendant of) Perseus (the founder of Mycenae, and the hero who beheaded the gorgon Medusa). Unbeknownst to Zeus, another child of that house was nearing its birth.

To ensure that the product of Zeus's infidelity would not become high king as intended, Hera went to Ilithyia, the goddess of childbirth, and tied Ilithyia's clothing in knots, her legs crossed. As no mortal could be born with Ilithyia in such a position without the intervention of a god, Heracles and his unborn twin half-brother were stuck in the womb of Alcmene.

Hera, in order to ensure the succession of another high king, caused the child Eurystheus to be born prematurely. He was now the one destined to become the high king while Heracles and his brother remained unborn.

Hera never intended for Heracles to be born at all. It was when one of Alcmene's servants came to Ilithyia and lied to the goddess, saying that the twins had indeed been born. Ilithyia, overcome by surprise, reacted with such a startled gesticulation at the news that her bonds were broken, thus allowing the twins to be born.

Alcmene offered up the child Heracles in an attempt to escape the goddess's wrath, however, when he was brought before her by Athena, Hera didn't know the child's identity. She nursed him, but the child's incredible strength caused Hera pain while nursing.

She removed the suckling child from her breast (the milk coming out to form the Milky Way).

Though Hera cast the child aside, he had consumed some of the milk, and with that, he acquired his powers. He was brought back to the house of Alcmene, and would be raised by them. Still fearing Hera's wrath, the child (who had originally been named Alcides by his mortal parents) was renamed Heracles.

This was not to be the end of Hera's attempts on the boy, however. When he was less than one year old, Hera sent two snakes to kill the young Heracles. Although his brother cowered, Heracles took the beasts to be playthings. He strangled them and played with them in his crib.

Heracles would grow to adulthood and marry a woman named Megara. The two had children, and life was good until Hera decided to intervene yet again. Sources differ upon exactly when, but what is consistent is that Hera caused Heracles to go insane. He believed that he was being attacked by evil spirits. He fought back against these dark beings, the battle ending in their easy slaughter. The problem was, these were no demons. In his madness, he had killed his children (in some myths he also killed Megara, however others have her departing and marrying his charioteer and nephew Iolaus).

Just as he was about to kill his mortal pater Amphitryon, Athena, known for her protectiveness of heroes, cast a stone into Heracles's chest, causing him to lose consciousness.

Now guilty of a sin which would require absolution, Heracles went before the oracle of Delphi, not knowing that the oracle was under the influence of his evil step-mother (history has a lot of those) Hera. The oracle advised Heracles to go before the high king and serve him in whatever way he should require. If he did so, Heracles was promised immortality, and a seat at Olympus.

The high king Eurystheus, an ally of Hera, was all too eager to have such a mighty servant. Although Eurystheus originally said that the debt of Heracles would be considered cleansed after performing ten heroic tasks, his requirements of the budding hero would come to be known as the twelve labors of Heracles.

The first labor was to kill the Nemean Lion, a ferocious beast with nearly impenetrable skin. Not only this, he was given only thirty days to complete the task. Let's just say Heracles and Eurystheus had issues. Heracles gathered arrows in order to slay the lion but the arrows bounced harmlessly from the lion's tough hide. Stories differ on whether he was finally able to strangle the lion to death, or whether he shot an arrow through the lion's mouth. Regardless, Heracles had indeed passed his first test.

Heracles tried to skin the lion, but could not break through its thick skin. It was only when Athena guided him to use the lion's own claws, that he was able to achieve the task. Heracles skinned the lion, and fashioned a cloak of armor from its impenetrable hide.

The king, upon seeing Heracles returning and carrying the dead beast on the thirtieth day, was petrified. He forbade Heracles to enter the city again, and communicated the remainder of the tasks through use of a messenger.

The second labor of Heracles was to slay the Lernaean Hydra, a nine headed serpent. The hydra was spawned by Hera (surprise, surprise) in order to kill Heracles. Slaying the beast would prove to be an even more difficult trial than the Nemean lion.

The Bibliotheca (fallaciously attributed to Apollodorus) gives a detailed account of the bout. The hydra *began* with nine heads, poisonous breath and even its tracks could kill a man. Heracles covered his mouth and nose to protect himself from the miasma of poisonous gas.

Heracles quickly went to work, decapitating the heads of the hydra one-by-one. Much to his dismay, however, with every beheading, the hydra would sprout two to replace the stump. He called for his charioteer (some say nephew) Iolaus for help. A new approach was developed including both of the men. Heracles would sever each head, and Iolaus would quickly cauterize the stump before two new heads could be sprouted.

This method worked quite effectively, although Hera wasn't done yet. She sent forth a crab to distract Heracles so that the hydra would be able to defeat the hero. Heracles, undaunted, stomped the crab beneath his foot.

The final head of the hydra became immortal, however Heracles was able to sever it with the use of a golden sword which Athena had given to him. The beast was slain. Heracles, always an opportunist, dipped the tips of his arrows in the blood of the poisonous blood of the hydra.

Unfortunately for Heracles, upon completing his tenth task, Eurystheus declared the slaying of the hydra improperly completed as the hero had the help of his nephew and charioteer.

The third task of Heracles was to be different. Heracles had proven himself against the fiercest of Hera's creations, and so Eurystheus set the next task to be the capturing of the Ceryneian Hind, an animal sacred to Artemis, able to outrun an arrow.

Heracles awoke one morning to glimpse the light reflected from one of its antlers. He gave chase to the animal, but it was indefatigable. He would chase it for the space of one year.

He eventually caught it, but on his return was confronted by Artemis and her brother Apollo. Heracles quickly explained and apologized for the situation. Artemis agreed to forgive him, so long as he let it go upon proving the hind's capture. Heracles agreed and, upon reaching the gates of the city, insisted that Eurystheus come and behold the animal for himself.

When Eurystheus came outside the city gates, Heracles, true to his promise let the hind go. He taunted Eurystheus, saying that the king had been too sluggish, and that it was his fault that the hind had escaped. It's not like the two were friends, but Eurystheus became more determined than ever to foil the hero's quest to become immortal.

The fourth labor of Heracles was to capture the Erymanthian Boar. He consulted a centaur for guidance, and was told to lead the boar into thick snow. By these means, he was able to capture the animal. He returned to the centaur. The centaur was overcome with fear at the sight of it. He begged Heracles to dispose of the boar, and Heracles obliged.

As the fifth labor, Eurystheus decided to not only present Heracles with a near impossible task, but to humiliate him in the process. The fifth labor was to clean the stables of Augeas in one day. Augeas, no doubt excited to learn that his stables would finally be cleaned, offered Heracles one-tenth of his herd, should the hero be able to finish the job in the space of a day.

While certainly being demeaning work, Eurystheus felt that the labor would be futile, as the stable housed over a thousand immortal cattle which produced an epic amount of droppings. To add further difficulty, the stables had not been cleaned in over thirty years.

Heracles, always persistent, rerouted two rivers, the Peneus and the Alpheus to run through the stables, thus washing them clean. Augeas, thinking the task impossible in such a short time-frame, rescinded his offer to the hero, claiming that he had already been instructed to carry out the cleaning anyway. In many myths, upon completion of his labors, Heracles would return to kill the reneging stable-owner.

After his tenth labor was complete, Eurystheus would declare this task to be forfeit as the slaying of the hydra, due to the fact that it was not Heracles, but the rivers which cleaned the stables.

The sixth labor of Heracles was to kill or drive away the Stymphalian birds. These, true to form, were no ordinary birds, but creatures with bronze beaks, and

metallic feathers which the birds could use as projec-
tiles to fend off any possible predators. And, as if
Heracles hadn't waded through enough feces, the
droppings of the birds were poisonous.

Heracles went to the swamp where the birds dwelled,
however, he was unable to make his way closer to
them as he would sink in the soft ground. Athena
came to the rescue once again, presenting Heracles
with a rattle, made by Hephaestus. Upon shaking it,
the birds were frightened and took wing. He killed
many of them with his bow, while the rest would fly
away.

The seventh labor was to capture, but not kill, the
Cretan bull. This bull had been causing all sorts of
havoc in Crete. The king of the time (mythical King
Minos) was quick to offer his aid, but Heracles refused. He was able to come up behind the bull and
beat it to within an inch of its life.

He had the bruised and beaten bull sent back to Eurystheus who intended to sacrifice it to Hera. The
goddess, however, refused the sacrifice, and Eurystheus let the beast go.

The eighth labor was to capture Diomedes's horses.
The task may have seemed simple at first, but Heracles soon came to the knowledge that the mares were
wild, likely caused by a steady diet of human flesh.

Diomedes was hardly keen to have his horses taken. In a common version of the myth, Heracles refused to sleep during the night, fearing that Diomedes would try to kill him in his sleep. He snuck in and severed the chains which held the horses.

He then spooked them to the top of a peninsula, took his axe and cut the land around the peninsula and thus trapped the horses on his self-made island. Heracles killed Diomedes and fed him to his horses which calmed the man-eaters down enough for the hero to bind their mouths and return them to Eurystheus.

The ninth labor was a task for the petulant king's petulant daughter. She coveted the girdle of Hyppolyta, the queen of the Amazons, and so her father Eurystheus commanded the retrieval of the belt to be the ninth labor.

Heracles set sail with some of his companions and, upon landing on the shores of the Amazon's territory, told the Amazonian queen of his task. The queen was impressed, and offered to give the girdle to Heracles without protest, even though it had been a gift to her by the god of war Ares.

Hera, however, just couldn't stay out of things, and disguised herself, slandering Heracles to the Amazons. She told them that his real purpose was to kidnap their queen and the Amazons quickly attacked him and his ship.

Heracles fought off the Amazons, killing their queen and taking the girdle from around her. He set sail, and delivered the belt to Eurystheus.

The tenth labor (which was supposed to be his last) was for Heracles to return with the cattle of the monster Geryon. This task was in a far off land, and so Heracles had to do some traveling.

He reached the desert of Libya and, while trudging through it, became angry at the excessive heat. To vent his displeasure, he shot an arrow at Helios, the Titan who carried the sun through the sky. While the arrow missed its target, Helios was so impressed by the feat that he offered his golden cup to assist Heracles in his travels through the desert. This cup was the means of by which Helios made his conveyance from the west (at the end of the day) to the east (to begin the next day). By using this cup, Heracles was able to reach the land of Erytheia where Geyron and his cattle lived.

Upon disembarking, Heracles encountered a two-headed dog named Orthrus. He made short work of the animal, killing it with his club. The herdsman in charge of the cattle tried to join Orthrus in fending off the hero, but was himself slain.

Alerted by the sounds of fighting, Geryon sprang into action. The monster, depending on the source, either had three heads and one body, or one head and three bodies, either two or six legs; various combinations of Geryon's anatomy are recorded.

The monster donned his armor and set off to attack Heracles. The hero, however, shot Geryon with one of his hydra-poisoned arrows with a force that sent the arrow through the monster's forehead, killing him.

Now at his leisure, Heracles collected the cattle and traveled back to Eurystheus. In one version of the story, the cattle are stolen by a giant named Cacus while Heracles is sleeping. The giant dragged the cattle backward so as to confuse the hero, should he go looking for them.

Heracles would find the trail, finding a cave with an enormous stone set in front of it (by Cacus). Heracles, quite the strong figure himself simply tore the top from the mountain and did battle with the giant. He slayed his foe, but Hera turned herself into a gadfly and proceeded to bite the cattle, causing them to scatter. Over the space of a year, Heracles would find all of the cattle, and so he made his way back to Eurystheus, thinking it to be for the last time.

Eurystheus, however, rejected two of the labors (the killing of the hydra and the cleaning of the stables), and insisted that Heracles was not yet finished. He therefore set two more tasks ahead of the hero.

The eleventh labor of Heracles was to gather the golden apples from the garden of Hesperides. The Hesperides were nymphs who tended the garden where the golden apples grew. According to one myth, these golden apples would grant the one who ate of them immortality for the space of one day. An individual could, in theory, eat an apple a day and become immortal. (There's a rhyme in that somewhere).

Upon reaching the garden, Heracles came across Anteus, a being who was immortal unless he was separated from his mother Gaia. Heracles, upon discovering this, lifted his foe from the ground and crushed him in his strong arms.

Heracles reached the garden, but was unable to retrieve the apples on his own. He went to Atlas, the Titan holding up the sky, and made a deal with him. Heracles would hold up the sky and Atlas would receive a rest from his duties for the time it took the Titan to retrieve the apples (I think we see where this is going). Atlas quickly agreed and Heracles took to holding Uranus from Gaia.

Upon Atlas's return, however, the Titan refused to return to his post. Heracles, not willing to give up his quest and acquiesce to being the new form of separation between the sky and the earth, tricked Atlas into resuming his duty by asking the Titan if he would hold the sky long enough for Heracles to adjust his cloak. Atlas agreed (and I think we see where this one's going too) and Heracles quickly made off with the apples.

The hero returned, giving Eurystheus the golden apples, ready for his twelfth and final labor.

The twelfth labor of Heracles was to capture, but not kill Cerberus, the three-headed dog which guarded the underworld. Heracles was also not allowed to use any weapons in the tri-headed dog's capture.

The hero set out. He went to Eleusis in order to gain the knowledge of how to enter and exit the underworld while retaining his life. With the help of Hermes and Athena, he was able to enter the gates of the underworld at Tanaerum. He traversed the river Styx and, upon arriving in the underworld, opened up a dialog with Hades.

Hades agreed to allow Heracles to take Cerberus so long as he could capture the dog(s) without hurting him, and return the guardian dog(s) safely after the labor was complete. Heracles agreed.

Either before or after his conversation with Hades, Heracles came upon two men who were bound to chairs in the underworld. The men were Pirithious and Thesius, two men who had endeavored to kidnap Persephone so that Pirithious could take her as his wife.

Heracles was able to wrest Thesius from his chair, leaving a portion of the latter's thigh. Heracles was unsuccessful freeing Pirithious, however. It was said that the attempt shook the earth.

Heracles would finally come upon Cerberus. He was able to capture the Cerberus and didn't harm the dog in the process. He took Cerberus before Eurystheus, but when the king beheld the guardian of the under-world, he is said to have died of fright. (According to some myths, he simply cowered and told Heracles to return the dog to the underworld). Regardless what happened to Eurystheus, Heracles was now free of his debt for killing his children (and possibly wife).

The journey of Heracles was far from over, but he was finally free.

CHAPTER **12**

Other Important Beings in Structure of Greek Mythology

The mythos of the Greeks was not limited to the major gods and the demigods (such as Heracles). A number of other characters would find an important role in the belief system of the ancient Greeks.

Prometheus was the most important character in regard to humankind, for he was their creator. The son of the Clymene and the Titan Iapetus, Prometheus did not participate in the direct conflict between the Titans and the Olympian gods (in other versions, he fought on the side of the Olympians). He was, therefore, spared their fate.

Prometheus fashioned the first human beings out of clay or mud and showed his creations to the goddess Athena. The goddess was so impressed that she breathed life into them. Thrilled by his creations being given life, Prometheus would teach the humans everything that he knew of math, science, and civilization. This would cause the first rift between Zeus and Prometheus.

Zeus, upset by Prometheus's indiscretion of teaching the humans the knowledge of the gods, made humankind mortal and cast them away from Mount Olympus.

At a dinner between gods and mortals, Prometheus presented Zeus with an option of two meals. One meal was that of an ox (unbeknownst to Zeus, Prometheus had set a meal of beef in the stomach of the ox), the other was that of gleaming fat (beneath which, Zeus would find only bare bones). Zeus, tantalized by the fatty plate, chose it as his meal. When he discovered that the plate was made up of bones which had been stripped of their meat, Zeus became furious with Prometheus.

Prometheus also gave humans fire. Accounts differ as to whether the humans already had the use of fire, but were stripped of it after Prometheus's fat and bones trick on the king of gods, or whether they didn't have fire in the first place. What is common though, is that Zeus at one point forbade the humans to be allowed the use of fire.

Seeing his creations suffering, Prometheus stole away the fire of the gods which Zeus had hidden and presented it to the humans, giving them (or returning to them) the use of flame.

For this, Zeus would levy one of his most extreme punishments. He had Prometheus chained to a rock where every day an eagle (a symbol of Zeus) would devour his liver. At night, the liver of Prometheus would regrow, allowing this cycle to continue on eternally.

Depending on the version of the myth, Prometheus was never freed from his bondage or, in some versions, was unchained by Heracles.

Perseus and Medusa

Medusa is, no doubt, one of the most familiar figures from Greek mythology. What is often not known about her is that she was once a stunningly beautiful, virginal priestess of Athena, the goddess of war and wisdom.

As Athena was a virgin, so too were all of her priestesses. Medusa had many suitors, but always held firm to her oaths of chastity. It was not only mortal men, however, that found Medusa irresistible.

The god Poseidon came to Medusa while she was inside Athena's temple on the hill of the acropolis. He viciously attacked and raped her. The act was not only a heinous violation of the young priestess, but a sacrilege to Athena.

Athena, however, did not take the side of her priestess. For the crime of *being* raped, Athena placed a terrible curse upon Medusa. Her skin was cracked and aged, her beauty turned to hideousness, her long hair was transformed into snakes and all who looked upon her would be turned to stone. Medusa was transformed into a gorgon.

Medusa was cast into exile, but quickly became hunted. According to the myth, even after Medusa was slain, her head would still cause any who looked upon her to turn to stone. Warriors came from all around to capture this tactical prize, only to be turned to stone in Medusa's growing rock garden.

Medusa would meet her match, however, at the hands of a warrior named Perseus. Danaë, the mother of Perseus, had been locked into a stone tower by her father Acrisius, the king of Argos. With no male heir, Acrisius consulted an oracle to discover whether his daughter would bear a grandson. The oracle instructed Acrisius that if Danaë were to become pregnant, her son would one day kill him and take his throne.

The theme of the older generation fearing their overthrow by a younger generation has persisted throughout the world, not only in myth and culture, but in real life as well.

Acrisius, fearing his as yet unconceived grandson, locked Danaë into the stone tower, expecting her to die from starvation as she was given very little food. The one thing that Acrisius hadn't prepared for, however, was the attention of the gods.

Zeus, always the philanderer, came through the window as a shower of gold. He impregnated Danaë with a son. When the news of his daughter's death never came, Acrisius went to investigate, finding his daughter holding her newly born child Perseus.

Afraid of offending Zeus, he didn't dare kill the two outright; however, he placed Danaë into a boat and set her adrift in the sea. They would eventually land on the island of Serifos. As Perseus grew, the king of Serifos became enamored with his mother. Hating Perseus, the king demanded that all occupants of Serifos provide him with a lavish gift; those who did not would be banished.

As Perseus was poor, the king expected him to be unable to present a fitting gift. In order to prevent the king from taking his mother as his wife and banishing him, Perseus promised the king that he would bring as his offering the head of Medusa.

The problem for Perseus was that he not only lacked any weapons, armor or knowledge of what Medusa looked like (as any who had actually seen her form would have been turned to stone), he also had no idea where he was going.

He prayed to the gods and, having heard his prayer, Zeus sent forth Hermes who gave the young man a pair of winged sandals. Hermes then told Perseus of a group of nymphs who would help him further. In order to find the nymphs, Perseus had to confront the Graeae, sisters of the gorgons.

The Graeae were three beings who shared use of one eyeball. In order to gain their cooperation, Perseus snatched the eyeball from the sisters and demanded that they tell him how to reach the grove of the nymphs. This was the same garden which Heracles encountered while searching for the golden apples.

Upon reaching the grove, the nymphs gave him a satchel within which Perseus could store the severed head of Medusa without fear of being turned to stone. Before he reached Medusa though, he would require much more.

He gained the necessary items by the kindness of the gods. Hades provided Perseus with a helm of darkness; Zeus gave Perseus an adamantine sword; and Athena gave Perseus the polished shield which would become iconic of the hero.

Now very well prepared for the confrontation, Perseus traveled to the island where Medusa had been exiled. By walking backward, he was able to view Medusa by looking at her reflection through the polished shield that Athena gave to him. By this means, he was able to sneak up on her and cut off her head.

When Perseus returned to the island of Serifos, he found his mother about to be married to the king against her will. The king had been making violent advances toward Danaë, and so Perseus, always protective of his mother used Medusa's head on the foul king. Acrisius had also come to attend the wedding and, justly enough, he too caught a glimpse of the gorgon's head.

Perseus would eventually offer Medusa's head to Athena as a tribute.

The Minotaur

Son of a human mother and a bull father, the Minotaur was one of the most feared of all the monsters in
ancient Greece. Residing in a labyrinth on the island
of Crete, the Minotaur lied in wait for a prisoner to
enter its dwelling. Once found, the victim would be
torn limb from limb and devoured by the ravenous
beast.

The Minotaur was brought into being by an offense
toward the god Poseidon by the king of Crete, Minos.
The king had prayed to Poseidon to send a white bull,
showing him favor and as the rightful heir to the
throne of Crete. Upon its arrival, Minos had promised
to sacrifice the bull to Poseidon; however, having become an admirer of the beauty of the bull, Minos re-
neged. (In another version of this story, Minos would
slaughter the most prized new calf every year to Poseidon, but when the white bull was born, he couldn't
bring himself to sacrifice it. Instead he slaughtered
another bull, thinking that the god would call it
even).

What is consistent in the myths is Poseidon's reaction
to the sleight. He caused Minos's wife, Queen
Pasiphaë to fall in love with the bull. The queen
longed to copulate with the beast. She commissioned

a great inventor named Daedalus to build her a wooden cow, hollow on the inside.

The queen took the decoy into the pasture where the bull lived, climbed inside and the rest is best left to the imagination. She became pregnant and, upon her delivery, the Minotaur (or bull of Minos) was born.

In an effort to turn lemons into lemonade, Minos decided to use the Minotaur to his own advantage. He commissioned Daedalus to envision and build a prison wherein the Minotaur would be placed, and any prisoners would be forced to face it.

Androgeus the son of Minos was in Athens, competing in Panathenaic Games, an early predecessor to the Olympics. He won every event, angering the other competitors. These men killed him. When Minos heard of this, he declared war on Athens.

In lieu of a full on attack, Minos demanded that seven male virgins and seven female virgins be offered to him as tribute to be sacrificed to the Minotaur once every nine years. This repeated until the third cycle when Theseus, son of not only the king and queen of Athens, but of Poseidon as well.

Having this dual paternity allowed Theseus to be an heir to the Athenian throne and also possess some of the powers of the gods. When he grew, the third set of virgins was rounded up, and he joined with them, vowing to bring down the terrible beast which had killed those sent before him. Having grown enough to retrieve his father's sword from beneath a boulder (where Aegeus, the king of Athens and father of Theseus had placed it), Aegeus had only one request of his son. Should he survive and return home, he should raise the white sail instead of the black sail in order to show his father that he lived.

When Theseus arrived at Knossos, the capitol of Crete, he quickly caught the eye of Ariadne, the daughter of king Minos. She fell in love with him and went to Daedalus in order to find some way to help the young man return from his imprisonment in the labyrinth. Daedalus gave her a clue (or ball of string) so that she could offer Theseus a way back to the entrance of the maze. She had one condition though. If Theseus survived, he would have to agree to marry her. Theseus agreed.

The fourteen virgins were led the next morning to the entrance of the labyrinth and locked inside. With his ball of twine, Theseus would lead the way. He bore the sword of Aegeus, and made his way in the dark through the labyrinth, searching for the Minotaur.

By the time his clue was one-quarter the size it had been upon his entry, Theseus comes across the sleeping Minotaur. Theseus ambushes the bull-headed creature, catching him off guard. The two would do battle: the Minotaur wielding an axe, Theseus with a sword.

The two do battle, but Theseus quickly has the upper hand. He corners the Minotaur and is able to slay him, but he's not out of the woods yet. Day is approaching and, should Theseus and the other virgins be caught by king Minos, they will surely be slain. He quickly makes his way back through the labyrinth, following the string that Ariadne had given him. Theseus and the others would escape in the dark of the night. Before dawn arrived, Ariadne met Theseus on the Athenian's boat and the group set sail toward Athens.

Aegeus, Theseus's father, had gone to a cliff overlooking the sea every day in order to ascertain his son's fate. When the ship came into view, Theseus had neglected to raise the white sail. Aegeus, thinking his son to be dead was so distraught that he cast himself over the cliff and to his death. These waters would come to be called the Aegean Sea.

CHAPTER 13

Greek Mythology and Homer's Iliad and Odyssey

Before ending, the myths and legends described by Homer in Iliad and Odyssey bear some investigation.

The stories of Homer's Iliad and Odyssey were originally communicated through word of mouth by travelling bards. They were collected by Homer (and possibly altered to fit into Homer's own sense of the story). While a brief synopsis of each will be given here, I also encourage you to read these two epics. They have been an inspiration in culture and literature since their original telling, over 2,500 years ago.

Iliad

Homer's Iliad begins near the end of the Trojan War. The Achaeans (or Greeks) are battling the Trojans. A priest of Apollo offers Agamemnon, the king of the Achaeans, vast wealth in exchange for Agamemnon to return his daughter Chryseis. Agamemnon refuses.

The priest then prays to Apollo for help and guidance and the god, a patron of Troy, sends forth a plague into the Greek camp which claims many lives. This plague continues for the space of nine days, until Achilles, hero of the Greeks and leader of the legendary Myrmidons, demands that Agamemnon return the girl to her father and end the plague.

While Agamemnon agrees to return Chryseis, he takes Briseis, a captive of Achilles, as recompense. Achilles is enraged and from that point refuses to fight. He also orders his Myrmidons to stand down. They threaten to leave the battle and the beach near Troy altogether. Meanwhile, Odysseus returns Chryseis to her father, thus ending the plague on the Greeks.

Mutinous, Achilles bids his mother Thetis, a goddess of the sea, to beseech Zeus and ask him to fight on the side of the Trojans. He does this in order to either convince Agamemnon to appreciate how much he needs Achilles and his Myrmidons, or bring a swifter end to the war. Zeus agrees, and the tide is turned.

Agamemnon has a dream that night, sent by Zeus, instructing him to attack the city walls. Upon his awakening, Agamemnon decided to test the morale of his soldiers by telling them all to head home. With the recent plague and the refusal of Achilles and his Myrmidons to fight, the soldiers were very nearly routed. It was only by the intervention of Athena, through the mouth and actions of Odysseus that the Greeks remained. He challenged and killed a discontented soldier for airing his grievances about the continued combat.

Word of the Greeks' pending attack reaches Priam (king of Troy) who then sets his own men out to the battlefield. As the armies approached each other, Paris, the prince of Troy and man who had stolen Helen from the Greek Minelaus, the act which purportedly started the war, (see previous chapter's section regarding Paris and the three goddesses), offered to fight a duel with the vastly superior warrior Minelaus to decide the victor of the war. Paris was no match for Minelaus, but was spared by Aphrodite before he could be killed.

At the intervention of Zeus, an arrow takes flight and wounds Minelaus, thus breaking the temporary truce and rejoining the battle. One of the great warriors on the side of the Greeks is Diomedes. He kills many soldiers, including Pandaros, the man who released the arrow wounding Minelaus. Aphrodite intervenes, but is wounded by Diomedes. Apollo then comes forth and warns Diomedes against battling against the gods, but the latter is not dissuaded.

The gods of Olympus were split in regard to their support of the armies, and Diomedes wounds yet another deity, Ares, who shrieks out in a very un-war-god-like cry (see above section on Ares).

After rallying his forces, Hector (brother of Paris and prince of Troy) reenters the city to bid the people toward prayer and sacrifice. He returns to the battle and confronts Ajax, a mighty Greek warrior. The two fight to a stalemate as the sun goes down.

The next day, the two armies agree to a day's peace so that they can burn their dead. The Greeks also erect a wall for protection. Paris refuses to return Helen over the protestation of many of the Trojans. He offers instead to return a treasure he had stolen and much of his own riches, but this offer is in vain.

Upon the next morning, the gods are forbidden by Zeus to interfere in the battle. The Trojans are victorious on the day and drive the Greeks back to their encampment. The sun goes down and prevents the Trojans from assailing the walls, so instead, they camp on the field.

Meanwhile, Agamemnon is ready to do whatever necessary to convince Achilles to return to the battle. He sends two heralds along with the Greek warriors Odysseus, Phoenix and Ajax who also bear gifts to Achilles. The Myrmidon warrior refuses to return to battle unless the Trojans breach the Greek walls and attack their camps and ships with fire.

During the night, Diomedes and Odysseus kill a Trojan warrior and generally cause mayhem among the camps of the Trojan allies. When morning comes, Hector leads the charge against the Greeks. He is begged not to proceed by Polydamas, an oracle, but the prince continues onward.

Zeus, who had continued to prohibit the gods from interference, is lured to sleep by Hera so that Poseidon can intervene on the side of the Greeks. Upon waking, Zeus sends forth Apollo on the side of the Trojans to sway the tide of the battle back in the favor of the Trojans. Unfortunately for the Trojans, they reach the ships and cause Achilles to send his friend Patroclus into battle wearing his armor to rally the Greek soldiers.

The tide of the battle is again turned, and Patroclus kills one of the Trojan heroes, sending the Trojans into retreat. He pursues the Trojans back to the city walls and is confronted by Apollo himself. Patroclus is killed by Hector, thinking the warrior to be Achilles.

Hector takes the armor of Achilles as his own and chaos breaks out.

The news of his slain friend is enough to enrage Achilles. He swears vengeance on the prince of Troy and he stands at the gate of the Grecian walls and, inspired by Athena, thunders in rage at the Trojan army. The Trojans are terrified by the presence of Achilles and in the cacophony, the Greeks are able to retrieve the body of Patroclus, and they bring his remains back to their camp.

New armor is fashioned by Hephaestus, and Achilles dons the gifts, ready to avenge his friend by killing the Trojan prince Hector. The next morning comes, and Agamemnon again offers Achilles gifts, including the return of Briseis, but Achilles has only one thing on his mind: his revenge on Hector.

Though Achilles is aware that he is destined to die young, and is even warned by his horse of his own coming death, the warrior drives his chariot into battle. He slaughters the Trojans before him and, splitting off about half of the Trojan forces, proceeds to slaughter this entire group. He is confronted by the river god Skamandros, who is upset that Achilles had littered his waters with so many dead Trojans. The god is driven back, however and Achilles returns to battle.

The gods, having been released by Zeus from their bonds of non-interference, rejoin the battle. Achilles is tricked by the god Apollo and led away from the mass of the Trojan forces as they retreat into the city. Only Hector remains outside the city walls.

Despite his initial urge to stand and fight, as Achilles draws closer, Hector begins to run around the walls of Troy, trying to evade the hero. He runs until Athena intervenes, fooling the prince into facing Achilles. The battle doesn't last long.

Achilles ties Hector's body to the back of his chariot and drags the prince's corpse back to the Greek camp. Despite being visited in a dream by his friend Patroclus who urges Achilles to bury Hector and allow the usual honors to fall to the slain prince, Achilles continues to desecrate the body by riding it around the funeral pyre of Patroclus.

Having had enough of this, Zeus sends Hermes to bring Priam to the tent of Achilles. Though initially confused by the Trojan king's presence, Priam's pleas compel Achilles to release Hector's body to the king. It is with the funeral of Hector that Homer's Iliad comes to an end.

Odyssey

The chronology of Iliad and Odyssey skips a number of years and a few important events which bear a mention albeit brief here. The city of Troy would fall to the Greek soldiers after Odysseus hatched a cunning plan during the funeral games for Hector, son of Priam.

The idea was to build a great wooden horse and present it as if it were a gift to the Trojans, honoring the god Poseidon. The Trojans brought the horse through their gate and into the city. Now unhindered, the Greeks only needed to wait until nightfall to spring from inside the horse and overtake the city.

The plan worked nearly to perfection; however, Paris, the one who caused the war and who cowered before Minelaus, shot Achilles through the heel with a poisoned arrow, killing him. Alternatively, one version of the story has Paris stabbing Achilles in the back while the latter was being married to Polyxena, one of Priam's daughters. Either way, Paris's slaying of Achilles never bears him any honor, and Achilles goes to his grave having never been defeated in battle.

Homer's Odyssey begins ten years since the end of the Trojan War and Odysseus has yet to return to his native Ithaca where he is king. The Odyssey is told, quite often, through the use of flashbacks. When the text begins, he is actually near the end of his journey, but the text reveals the ins and outs of his travels and tribulations.

Back at home, his wife Penelope is constantly beset by one-hundred and eight different suitors. These men believe Odysseus to be dead, and are quick to pounce on the opportunity for free food, drink, and the chance to possibly become king of Ithaca.

Penelope, while she despises the suitors, is bound by convention to feed these vultures. She refuses to take one as her husband, but can't turn them away either.

Much of the first books which make up Homer's Odyssey involve Telemachus, the son of Odysseus and Penelope. Athena, Odysseus's greatest ally disguises herself and tells Telemachus to search for information about his father's fate. Athena also approaches Zeus around this time, conveniently when Poseidon is not around. She would further help the young man by securing a ship for him (disguised as Telemachus himself). She would also stand at his side while the young prince conferred with the townspeople about what should be done with the suitors.

Poseidon's hatred of Odysseus is one of the main themes, and certainly the main cause of the warrior and his men being so lost in their travels. The reasons behind this begin with Poseidon's siding with the Trojans in the war, and the false offering to the god in the form of the Trojan horse. However, this would only be the beginning of the sea god's hatred of Odysseus.

Telemachus would travel by ship to visit Nestor, one of the Greek warriors in the war against Troy, often considered to be the most respectable of the Greek warriors. He then travelled to Sparta and inquired of Minelaus and Helen (who had finally returned with her husband, thus rendering the Trojan War a needless conflict over a spousal affair). They told him that his father was most recently known to have been held captive on an island by the nymph Calypso.

Now the story shifts its focus to settle on Odysseus himself. Odysseus is indeed entangled by the nymph Calypso who, having fallen in love with him, keeps him stranded on her island for the space of seven years. It's only when Hermes, intervenes that Calypso finally releases Odysseus. She gives him supplies as Odysseus builds a raft for himself.

Poseidon, still angered with Odysseus, sinks Odysseus's craft. Luckily, Odysseus had his share of allies throughout his plight, and he is obscured by the sea nymph Ino. He swims to shore, but has not only lost his craft, but his clothing as well.

He wakes on the shore, roused by the sounds of women laughing with each other. He comes out of the forest and discovers the princess Nausicaa and her maids washing their clothes in the sea. The servants flee in fear, but Odysseus beseeches Nausicaa to help him. She takes Odysseus in, giving him clothing and shelter.

While a guest of Nausicaa and the house of Scherie (the island upon which he had landed), a bard recounts two tales, one of the quarrel of Achilles and Odysseus, and the other about an affair involving Ares and Aphrodite. Odysseus, who at this point hadn't shared his identity with his hosts, asked the bard to recount the first tale. He exposes his identity by not being able to contain his emotions at the bard's words. It is from this point that Odysseus recounts his travels after the end of the Trojan War.

He began his trip home with twelve ships, carrying all of his men. They raided the city of Ismaros in Cicones. While Odysseus insisted that they leave quickly after dividing up the women and plunder, the men refused. The Cicones attacked the next morning, killing many of Odysseus's men. He and his remaining forces were able to escape, but they had their casualties.

Odysseus and his men would then come across lotus-eaters, lazy people who did nothing but eat lotus. The lotus-eaters didn't harm Odysseus or his men, but gave some of them lotuses to eat. The men who ate them no longer wanted to return home, rather, they stayed behind to gorge themselves with lotus.

Odysseus and his remaining men were then imprisoned by the Cyclops Polyphemus. Odysseus was eventually able to free himself by blinding the Cyclops, but made the mistake of telling Polyphemus his name. The Cyclops then entreated his father Poseidon (of course it had to be Poseidon).

Now filled with renewed rage toward Odysseus and his men, Poseidon put a curse upon Odysseus that he should wander the seas for the space of a decade.

Odysseus briefly came upon a hint of good fortune when they stayed with the master of the winds, a being named Aeolus. The master gave Odysseus a bag which contained the north, south and east winds. The ships came just in sight of Ithaca and everything was going well until one night while Odysseus was asleep, his men greedily opened the bag, thinking it to be treasure, and released all of the winds contained within. The resulting storm would carry the ships backward, far away from Ithaca. They found Aeolus again, but he refused to help them further.

The men set onward again, finally coming to the island of the Laestrygonians, a cannibalistic tribe. Odysseus's ship was the only one who didn't enter the harbor, and was thus the only one spared from complete destruction.

He would later run across the witch and goddess Circe. Having been warned about Circe by Hermes, Odysseus took a drug called moly which prevented what was about to happen to half of his men from happening to him. As the men ate and drank, they were turned into pigs. When Odysseus was able to resist the magic, Circe agreed to return his men to their original form provided that Odysseus would love her. They stayed on this island for a year, until Circe finally gave Odysseus the knowledge of how to contact the dead for guidance.

Odysseus traveled to an island on the western edge of the world and came across many spirits, including a crewman named Elpenor who asked Odysseus to find and bury his body. Odysseus agreed and was then visited by a prophet named Tiresias. Tiresias instructed Odysseus on how to return home without losing all of his men (not eating the sun god's flocks), and informed him that he had angered Poseidon by blinding his myopic son. He also came across Achilles, Agamemnon, Heracles, Minos, Orion, and other characters. He is eventually beset by innumerable souls from the underworld asking of news of their relatives. He retreats and leaves the island.

He returned to the island of Circe, who instructed them on the final stages of their journey. They sailed past the island of the sirens, women whose voices so entranced sailors that they steered their ships into the rocks. All of the men with the exception of Odysseus plugged their ears with bee's wax.

Next they sailed between the whirlpool Charybdis and the six-headed monster Scylla. Many of his men were lost, but Odysseus and his remaining companions made it through to safety. They would land on the island where the sun god's cattle resided. While Odysseus was asleep, all of his men chased down, slaughtered and ate the cattle. Upon their departure, the ships were wrecked, and all but Odysseus (the only one who hadn't partaken in the offense toward Helios) were killed.

He would come ashore the island of Calypso. The nymph fell quickly and deeply in love with Odysseus and forced him to remain with her until Zeus (via Hermes) demanded that he be released seven years after landing on the island; thus bringing the guests of Nausicaa up to speed.

The attendants of the party quickly agreed to help Odysseus get home. They set forth while Odysseus was sleeping and delivered him to a harbor in Ithaca where he goes on to find his own slave's quarters. Athena disguised Odysseus that he might view with anonymity the state of his house and kingdom. The slave, a swineherd named Eurnaeus, took him in and fed him.

After regaling the local farmers with a false tale about his disguised self, Odysseus comes across his own son Telemachus who had just returned from Sparta, narrowly evading an ambush by the suitors of Penelope. He discloses his identity to his son and the two set out to kill the suitors.

While in the house, being patched up, one of the maids washing his feet recognizes Odysseus's scar and runs off to tell the lady of the house. Athena intervenes, causing Penelope to be deaf to the woman's words.

Athena again intercedes by telling Penelope the following day to hold a competition where whosoever of the suitors could string Odysseus's bow and shoot an arrow through twelve axe heads could have her hand in marriage.

Odysseus joins the contest himself and is the only one capable of stringing the bow. He easily fires an arrow through the axe heads and along with his son, Athena, Eurnaeus and a cowherd he slaughters the suitors. They also hang a dozen maids who had slept with the suitors or deceived Penelope, along with a goatherd who had ridiculed Odysseus.

He finally reveals his identity to Penelope. She is at first skeptical, but when she tests him about what kind of bed they shared, he tells her accurately that it surrounds a living olive tree.

The next day, he meets with Laertes, his father, who only accepts that it's really Odysseus after the latter faithfully recounts the orchard which the former had gifted him. The story isn't quite over yet though, as the parents of the suitors set forth to take revenge on Odysseus. In her final intervention of the tale, Athena comes forth as Mentor (the disguise she had used while Telemachus was beseeching the people before his journey to Sparta) and causes them to forget their anger. Thus, the Odyssey is complete.

These large and profoundly beautiful volumes can be summed up, but hardly done justice outside of their own text. Their inclusion here is necessary, as is their inclusion in any text about Greek mythology, however, I again encourage you to read these phenomenal works for yourself.

CHAPTER 14

Meet Your Roman Doppelgangers

When Rome conquered Greece, rather than abolishing the Greek's religion, they, like many groups before and after including the Christians in Rome, ascribed the existing gods of the Greeks to aspects of their own mythology.

This was particularly easy for the Romans, as the Greek religion bore many similarities to their own, in fact, had likely inspired their own. The king of the gods in Greece, Zeus, would be attributed to the Romans' god Jupiter, a god of a similar nature. Ares would become Mars, Aphrodite would become Venus, Poseidon would become Neptune, Athena would become Minerva, and the list goes on.

The reason behind absorbing the religion of the Greeks rather than replacing it outright was simple. If conquerors take over your empire and strip you of your worship, they will be met with force and rebellion. In order to secure a more thorough and a much more peaceful transfer of power, the Romans would simply assimilate the gods and myths of the Greeks into their own system of belief.

This tactic has been used by conquerors and religious groups throughout the ages, notably by Christians. Once a powerful group, and no longer quite so persecuted in Rome, the Christians adopted the pagan holidays as their own. Although Christ is said to have been born in the summer or early fall, the Christians moved the date of his birth to be celebrated on December 25th, over the Roman pagan holiday of Saturnalia and also the birthdate of the Egyptian god Horus (among many others). Likewise, the festival of Easter which is celebrated as the resurrection of Christ is based off of the spring equinox and a pagan festival of fertility (and others). The festival celebrated Ishtar, a Babylonian goddess of fertility who was killed and resurrected.

By adapting the gods of the Greeks, the Romans ensured that the people would not rebel to nearly as great an extent over their rule. In fact, the Romans tended to respect the ancient Greeks and their manner of worship, and even added solely Greek legends and myths to their own pantheon.

This was quite out of character at the time for the Roman conquerors who often demanded more than simple fealty to the emperor. The Greeks were allowed to continue practicing their religion as they had done before this time.

CONCLUSION

Thanks again for downloading this book!

It has been a long journey. From Chaos to Heracles, from the birth of the Olympian gods to the Roman adaptation of the Greek religion, the culture and mythology of the Greeks never ceases to fascinate people from all over the world.

We have read of heroes and heretics, gods and men. The tales of Greek mythology are vast and intricate, describing not only the forces of nature, but the innermost being of the Greek people, indeed, of all people in their own inventive way.

The Greek perception of death is visited by the dreaded gorgon Medusa. Life is brought forth by Prometheus. Not to mention all of the trials of Odysseus as he searches for his way home.

In learning about other cultures, we learn not only about our past, but our present as well. There is a common thread within all of us, and that can be found in the way that we relate to each other. The world is often beset by troubled times, but there is always the opportunity to come together through understanding and a commonality which runs deeper than any disagreement or perceived difference.

Whether you read this text casually or for the purpose of gaining specific knowledge of the ideas, philosophies, myths and manners of the Ancient Greeks, I certainly hope that you found in this book the object of your intention.

It has been a great pleasure to share this wonderful collection of Greek myths with you, the reader, and I hope that you will join in further reading of the other books in this series. The other books in this series include a book regarding the history of ancient Greece, along with one book each of ancient Egypt's history and mythology. I hope to meet you again through the age-old sharing of ideas that is the connection between myth and history, science and religion.

Thank you,

Martin R. Phillips

PS. If you enjoyed this book, please help me out by kindly leaving a review!

35704221R00084

Made in the USA
Lexington, KY
21 September 2014